MORE POTTERIES LAD

Bill Ridgway

CHURNET VALLEY BOOKS
1 King Street, Leek, Staffordshire. ST13 5NW 01538 399033
www.leekbooks.co.uk
© Bill Ridgway and Churnet Valley Books 2010
ISBN 9781904546757
All rights reserved.
Any use of this book in any form needs the permission of both author and publisher.

It was August 1946, and we'd just been to see our new house being built at Chell. When we reached the crossing at Little Chell Lane we had to wait for Roger, one of the pit tankers, to chug back to Chatterley Whitfield

INTRODUCTION

It is more pressing than ever to record the recent past. There is no longer a casual acceptance that we will die where we were born, or even in the same country. Towns and villages which until recently had been occupied by generations of the same families are rare, as those affluent enough to leave the cities can soon outnumber the indigenous population. In time there will be no one left to say: this is what it was once like. Here was a mill, there a workhouse. Cities themselves are suffering from transient populations which make 'community' in the true sense of the word a thing of the past.

My memories are both personal and universal. My experiences are yours. You've lived through my times and my history is your mnemonic. It's a shared history, for we've all left footprints in the sand. It's also a requiem for a lost country; one that defined us both.

Lost, but not forgotten, for enough of the sounds and sights of my Potteries childhood are as real to me now as they were more than fifty years ago: children playing hop-scotch in the fading light; the clank of trains along the viaduct; the scrape of miners' boots; my fluttering home-made kite; the milkman's whistle and my mother's song. Voices, too: *Here comes the sun.... I'm pleased to tell you you've passed the examination.... Han thee gone yet, Ginny?* Words echo down the years, as clear now as when they were first spoken.

If we know nothing of our past, we face a rudderless future. This book is a celebration of that past - yours and mine.

Bill Ridgway 2010

The artwork throughout this book is by Adam

Was it forty years ago
I drove to Trentham on a whim?
Lesser pleasures to forgo,
For a rare al fresco swim.
Beyond the lake, and from the trees
Blew a resin-scented breeze

Motes and chalk-dust in a ray,
Thrown across initialled desks.
Turn up early on the day,
Be prepared to do your best.
Fifty years have passed since then -
Those blazered days and Parker pen

Searchlights over roof-tops loom,
Bombers rumble through the sky,
Steam trains thunder through the gloom,
As muffled up in bed I lie.
Now maypoles dance and thistles blow -
But that was sixty years ago

SECTIONS

1. Searchlights and Sirens   page   7
2. Kites, Dens and Dumps   page   41
3. A New Decade   page   81
4. Home and Away   page   117
5. Changing Times   page   153

6 More Potteries Lad

Tunstall 1940s.

1. SEARCHLIGHTS & SIRENS

Snapshot memories linger of war-time London, before my evacuation with my mother to Stoke-on-Trent. In the late summer dusk of 1943 I found myself on a train from Euston. It was packed with squaddies. The corridors were cramped with mis-shapen knapsacks, discarded coats and the paraphernalia of war. We squeezed into a crowded compartment and sat below a black and white railway photograph of Blackpool Tower. My mother had one of those old, battered suitcases fastened with a belt, and a soldier lifted the case down for her when we reached Stoke station. I was probably asleep during the bus journey to Tunstall, where we were to live with my father's parents in Lime Street. Less than a year later, we moved to his sister's hardly less cramped parlour in Pinnox Street. My London life had come to an end, my Potteries life just beginning.

Chapters

1. The Shelter
2. Locked in the Toilet
3. The Oatcake Man
4. Dolly Mixtures
5. Going Solo
6. Down the Overflow
7. A War-Time Wedding
8. The Minstrel and the Battleship
9. Starting School
10. Learning to Read
11. A Wasp in my Mouth
12. Distant Voices

Me starting at
St Mary's Infants
1945

1. THE SHELTER

Our rented house in Troutbeck Road, New Cross, London, had a roughly-grassed back garden and a trellis fence. Oddments of our war-time life lay scattered inside and out: my father's police helmet on a hall stand; a deckchair on a lawn flattened, rather than mown; windfall apples and brick-edged paths. My pedal-car was parked nearby. It had been painted in thick Post-Office red. When no air raid was imminent I'd take it on shopping expeditions with my mother.

I didn't mind the hard work, though steering was a problem. The Thames was a grey wash glimpsed between houses. A barrage balloon hung over the roofs. A khaki-clad soldier was explaining models of military vehicles to passers-by; brown lorries with canvas backs, tracked cars, vans and tanks. Then my mother's pace quickened and we had to get back.

There was much urgency then, and I knew it was to do with the monotone drone of the bombers which followed it, with my father at the doorway in his pyjamas, with the soldier and his models and the tethered balloon with its silver fins which hung over the water. I knew it was about air raid shelters, with the figures huddled to either side and the blanket I was wrapped in and the night sprinkled with sparks and blanched in searchlight beams. Distant booms were part of it too, and quakes which I could feel through the blanket though I knew they couldn't harm me because my mother was there.

Unarticulated anxieties kept pace with me and my pedal car. The air was shot with a strange agitation; the siren's wail, the fire-engine's bell, the overnight stubble on my father's face. Sometimes we were inside the house, booms and stutters faintly hammering at the blackout, a milk bottle shaking. Then the noises stopped, tea was made, everything was alright.

I was asleep when a blast shattered the bedroom window and blew the fireplace across the room. I have a vague memory of being on a dockside road when there was no barrage balloon and a German fighter came in low, strafing the street. A girl fell. My pedal car discarded, my mother wrenched open the door of a telephone box and I was inside and the plane had gone. But there were no bad dreams. And I was pedalling again.

A small hill of rough grass lay at the bottom of our garden. I couldn't climb it, so I ambled around it in my wellingtons. A scuffed patch led down a short slope to a door. There was mud, and I found I could make ambitious boot prints when I wasn't riding in my red car. At the back of the mound, near the lattice-fence, grey sheets of corrugated iron poked through the grass. The iron was damp, like the grass, and hard to the touch. My father sometimes slid back the door and I stood looking down into a dark cave with a bench and more mud with bigger footprints.

My mother had bought me a train book. It was hard-backed, and the pages were loose. Some were in colour, but most were line drawings. It was the first book I'd had. When I wasn't in my car I was looking at the cover, then looking at the pictures and trying to crayon them in. It was growing dark and I should have been in bed. I was crayoning instead, still crayoning as the sirens wailed and that ominous rumble began.

My mother was already buttoning my coat but that was less important than my book and crayons, which lay on the floor. The front door lay open, and I fumbled for my book but couldn't reach it because my mother had lifted me from the floor and my father was in the open doorway in his coat, a silhouette against the night sky. I wasn't going to leave without my book and crayons. I resisted, began to bawl.

Bombs were falling. There was a distant crump of shells, bells jangling. I'd reached my book and my mother snatched the crayons and now I was out in the open, the pages flying into the mud, the thuds nearer. My father was tugging at the shelter door. Now it was open and I was in that small, wet cave, crying for my lost book and the crayons trodden into the mud outside. The bombs were crashing and I was inconsolable. My treasured possession was somewhere else and my mum and dad didn't understand.

I hid myself in my mum's coat. She pulled a torch out of her pocket and offered it to me. I fiddled with the stud, unimpressed. A dank smell rose from the floor and a whiff of smoke drifted into the shelter. From time to time pale flashes came through cracks around the door. Then there was silence. And through the silence, the siren's mournful ululation, a sound which, like the roar of German bombers, I've never forgotten.

We left the shelter and walked through the muddy patch towards our house. And there were the dislodged pages, mud-smeared and crumpled, with my crayon packet and the remnants of crayons close by. My mother gathered them up. I found a wet stub, which I presented to her. I went inside still holding the coloured covers, and the tears had gone. It would all be put right. My mum would clean up the pages and stick them in and get new crayons and box them and then we wouldn't have to go into the Anderson again and the sirens wouldn't wail and the planes wouldn't drone and everything would be alright. And it was. Later we were in Euston Station, clambering on the train to Stoke, the sky hidden under an arch of opaque glass.

That was more than sixty years ago. This year, 2009, in one of those strange synchronicities of life, three things have happened: on a visit to a second-hand book shop in Suffolk, I discovered a copy of the tattered train book I carried to the shelter all those years ago. A few weeks later, watching the *Antiques Road Show*, I saw a model collection of the same war-time lorries and tanks I'd glimpsed as a child of three in a room by the Thames. Not long after, I was reading a letter sent to a daily paper from a reader who remembered the day the barrage balloons hadn't appeared in the London skies and the Focke-Wulfs came in low. The day my mother and I escaped their attention.

My first appearance. With Dad in the garden at our London home. Summer 1940

2. LOCKED IN THE TOILET

There was polished wood and grey glass windows. Some were high and open, so that the wheel-clicks came loudly into the corridor. Others were low, held by a leather belt which the soldiers pulled to let the windows fall before craning their necks into the darkness. There was steam too, and the black shape of a locomotive under a coaling tower.

It was a strange, moving world. A grey smoke billowed past Victorian villas, pale track-side lamps and unlit stations. The wheels beat a soporific tattoo over the points, and now the lamps and houses faded and the countryside was gliding past on a ghostly carousel..

My mother slid open the compartment door. 'Is there a seat in here?' There were more soldiers. Someone cleared a space. One of the squaddies lifted my mum's case on to the rack, and we sat, me on my mother's knee. There was a lot of talking, jokes between the soldiers, and through the window tenebrous fields slid past, their trees silhouetted against a pale sky.

One of the soldiers has sandy hair. Now he's delving into the pocket of his uniform. He takes out a notebook and pencil and starts to draw. He's drawn a locomotive, with steam gushing from the chimney and connecting rods at the wheels. He has a red pencil for some reason, and I'd never seen a red pencil before. He tears off the page and hands it to me, a red engine on a red track with a red driver looking out of a red cab and a red carriage behind it. 'Say thank you,' my mum chides, and I do, and stare at my wonderful red train and snatch a shy glimpse at the man who drew it. I like the drawing so much I need to go to the toilet to examine it in secret.

'You know where it is, just at the end of the corridor. D'you want me to come with you?'

'He's a big lad now,' says a squaddie. 'He'll be alright.'

I'm not sure, but I go anyway. The corridors are full of people and bags, and the train is swaying. I clutch my drawing and spot the door and go in. There's a basin and a toilet and I close the door behind me and notice the brass swivel. It must be a sort of lock, because I can turn it and shut the door tight. I sit on the seat and listen to the clatter of the real train and imagine the drawn train clattering too. I spend a long time imagining. Then I stuff my drawing into my pocket and try to get out.

The door is stuck. I can't move the swivel and I'm locked in. I fumble with it, try to move it but it's too stiff, won't budge. Somebody's at the door, trying to open it. I'm knocking on the door, panic rising, kicking it and pulling at the swivel.

'Are you alright in there?' It's a man's voice, maybe one of the soldiers in the corridor. He knocks again. 'Are you alright?'

'I'm locked in. I can't get out.'

The voice from the far side is muffled. The carriage sways, the toilet seems to have shrunk and I'm hemmed in. I might never get out again. 'My mum's down there somewhere. I can't undo it.'

'Have you turned the lock?'

'I can't get out. I'm locked in.'

'Which way are you turning the lock?'

'I don't know. My mum's in the carriage.'

'Turn it again. Turn it one way, and if that doesn't work, turn it the other.'

I'm in tears. He tries again, and this time I think there's someone else with him. 'Are you turning it?'

'It's stuck. I'm locked in.'

'Now, sonny, don't get upset. We'll get you out. Are you listening? Now try it the other way. Turn it around the other way.'

I do as he says. There's a slight click, and the man pushes the door open. 'You did it the wrong way, that's all.' It's the sandy haired soldier who drew my picture. 'Have you still got your train?'

I nod, wiping my eyes. 'I still got it.'

I walk back, found the compartment, took out my comforting drawing.

'You were a long time,' said my mum.

'I got stuck in.'

The blackouts were down, and the movement of the train and the wheel clicks sent me to sleep. Now we were coming to a stop. My mother was on her feet, her case handed down. I took a last furtive glance at our compartment from the corridor. The soldiers sat there motionless, saying words I couldn't hear behind the glass. The sandy-haired soldier gave me a wave. We were on the platform with our case and far ahead the engine sent up a thick cloud of steam which crept across the station canopy and vanished into the night sky.

The train began to move out.

'Where are we, mum?'

'We're at Stoke, now. Are you tired?'

'A bit.'

'We've got to get a bus to Tunstall.'

'Tunstall, what's that?' I hunted for my drawing, fell asleep again, opened my eyes. 'Wake up, Bill. We're here. We're going to see your grandma. And don't get locked in the toilet this time.'

A new life in the country for evacuees.

3. THE OATCAKE MAN

But now I'm walking from the Market Square with both parents. My memory has conflated more than one trip I made to the relative safety of my grandparents' Tunstall house before I came to Stoke for good. Sometimes, when bombing was heavy and my father was on police duty in Deptford, there was just me and my mother. But this time my father came too. He'd been buried under the rubble caused by a V1 explosion, and came back to his parents' house to recuperate. This was a separate journey, and there were three of us.

I'm walking in the dusk towards my grandparents' house. In my mind's eye I'm there twice, once as the boy outflanked by his parents, again as his doppelganger noting his familiar's progress from a street lamp behind. It's a close, sticky night. The streets are deserted, moths are fluttering under the gas-lamps. The flares throw a pallid nimbus across the pavement. It's very quiet, the only sound the ticking of the bus as we alight in the square, the shuffle of our cases along the backboard. It's downhill all the way from Market Street. We pass the Oddfellows' Arms, pass the cobbled alley to the rear of Woolworth's, then the old Police Station into John Street.

The road plunges sharply now, and as we begin our descent I see the shop. It's lit up, and it's this light I notice, because the houses surrounding it are in darkness. Why was it lit? What about the black-out? What about the war? There's a man behind the counter. He's wearing white, a white overall. He's holding something in his hand, a kitchen tool, something he uses on a kind of table. He's intent and doesn't see us. There's just him in the lit room, and the sweep of his hand as he uses the spatula, and we in the lamp-light walking past.

'D'you want an oatcake?' asks my dad.

I'm puzzled. 'What's an oatcake?' I ask him.

'I'll get us a couple.' He looks at my mother. 'Have you got the ration book?'

'Why, are they on ration?'

'I don't know.' He puts down his case on the pavement. My mother waits outside with it as we go in. My father says something to the man, and they confer with low voices. The man goes over to the window and lowers the blinds. Now he's bending over his griddle again, and I'm watching him pour something like milk from a basin, watching it form bright rings on the griddle, feeling its heat.

The puddles solidify. He lifts three with a deft action and drops them into a bag. My father pays and we leave and close the door behind us. 'Are they oatcakes, dad?'

'If they're not, they must be something similar. You can have some cheese on yours if your grandma's got some in.'

The explanation is half-understood, and I walk, tired, between the two. This is another place, different from London. We're walking past railings which enclose a grand building. It looks like a palace. I'm told it's where the Methodists go, and that has to do. The cases bump, we reach the cross-roads, a shop on opposite corners with no window-lights showing.

'Lime Street. We'll soon be there. Are you tired?' my mother asks.

Now there are no street lights, but the sky is blanching both roofs and road. At the bottom is the church I saw the last time I came, when the planes were droning in London. The church with the steeple. It's at the bottom of Lime Street with the steeple black against the lighter sky. The building is enormous against the small houses.

'St Mary's,' I say.

'You've got a good memory,' says my mum.

And we're at the door of my grandparents' house. My dad doesn't bother knocking. The door is always open, as are all the other doors in all the other streets. We go in with our cases, open the living room door. There's the clothes' strewn ceiling rack, the chaise-longue, the window overlooking the backyard, the grandmother clock, the stair door, the cellar door and the door you take when you want to go the 'back way'.

'I want a wee,' I announce.

' 'E wants go th' back way, Ginny,' my grandfather announces.

My grandma, always bustling, opens the door and I disappear down the yard. The sky is starry and still, and I hear the distant puff-puff of a train. I'm an *evacuee,* and I'm sure it's something to be proud of. I repeat it, because I like the sound. An evacuee, with a new address. It feels safe.

More than sixty years later, I remember the oatcake man in his lit shop surrounded by unlit houses. It seems a trivial thing to remember, far more trivial than being bombed out, which I've forgotten. But he's there, etched onto my early years along with other inconsequential fragments.

And I was lucky. My grandmother *did* have some cheese.

4. DOLLY MIXTURES

Now we were living in Pinnox Street, with Auntie Sib and Uncle Lou and my cousin Pat, for my grandparents' house already had too many occupants for a long stay. My father's three sisters, for a start. *Down* town was always from my grandparents house, whereas *up* town was from Auntie Sib's, and in either case you had to climb upwards to the High Street.

And going up town with my mother was an adventure. 'I'm just off to stretch my legs. Are you coming, Bill? Oh, I mustn't forget this -' taking the Ration Book off the mantelpiece. 'I'll not get far without it, will I?'

We'd take a short cut up Williamson Street, which ran parallel to Pinnox Street. Factory canyons reared up and there was often the whiff of smoke across the pavement. I'd catch a glimpse of Grindley's pot-bank barked in a century's toil, and old men in caps with the leathery skin of a gale-lashed Corsair, plodding to some unknown destination. This was the beginning of 'up town'.

The war-time High Street was the centre of my universe, and though it was as grim with grime as everywhere else, a sense of quiet excitement hung in the air. The road was sparse of lorries and vans. Very occasionally, there'd be a car. I came to associate rationing with this part of the city, with its air of restrained busyness, and the steady plod of war-time provincial life formed an image that lingered in my mind until, as a teenager, change finally arrived in luminous socks and beetle-crushers.

But that would be another episode. For now, lads still pedalled their delivery bikes, the contents of their baskets as limited as those in my mother's bag. And I wanted some dolly mixtures if they *had* any.

Dolly mixtures were just one of a range of items with which, even at an early age, I was familiar. Ovaltine, Nestle's Milk, Cod Liver Oil in its small square bottle and Tizer in its big brash bottle, Kia-Ora, dried eggs, Huntley and Palmer's biscuits, Wolseley socks, Moygashel rayons, Vim, Kolynos Dental Cream, Gibb's Dentifrice, Sifta Salt, Flit Fly Spray, Eno's Fruit Salts, Bird's Jelly, Dreen Shampoo, Yardley make-up - the war defined the list, the list the war, all under the umbrella of some ministry or other - the Ministry of Food, of Fuel and Power, the Ministry of Health. All collected from High Street shops when coupons allowed.

We were getting nearer to my Dolly Mixtures, but Frank Danby's shop was first on the list, or Boyce Adams, or Dewhurst's.

'I'm afraid the ration's down to 3oz of cheese, Mrs Ridgway.'

'Only 3 oz? I'd like to see my old man survive on 3 oz. Last time it was 8. I wish they'd make up their minds.'

'I've got a nice bit of liver just come in.'

'That's not on coupon, is it?'

'Not yet.'

'I'll take half a pound.'

'I can let you have a quarter.'

'Go on, then. Wrap it up.'

At least it wasn't Friday night, when the home-going potters would make a queue outside Woolworth's as news of new consignments spread and counter-girls were dispatched outside to break the news as stocks ran low.

'I bet you buggers 'n kept it under the counter for yourselves.'

'There might be some enamelware next week, but we can't be sure.'

'Enamelware? Thee castna' eat enamelware! What abite chocolates?'

Today there's no queue, and I'm heading for the sweets' counter, with Cherry Lips, Liquorice Root, Liquorice Allsorts, Harehound Liquorice, Liquorice Torpedos, Pontefract Cakes, Uncle Joes, Pear Drops, Little Gems, Sherbert Dip, Kay-Li, all sold by the ounce or half ounce - even Walker and Hartley's Devon Toffee if you hit the right time. And thinly-cut ice cream from the block. And broken biscuits and watery orange juice, the reminders of war confined to the black-out curtains by the door, and *My mother dun told me* from a gramophone wound by a girl charged with selling sheet music.

And Dolly Mixtures, of course.

'They've got some, mum. Have you got the coupon?'

'You can only have 2 oz. And you'll have to share with Pat.'

My Dolly Mixtures cascade onto the scales, then into a paper bag, which the girl seals with a swinging action. Coins are exchanged, coupons clipped out. I dip in my fingers, take out a couple of sweets, pop them in my mouth.

I'm all set for Askey's Fish Shop and Ball's Tobacconist's on the other side of the road when something so momentous happens it sidelines Woolworth's and the war and everything else I hear adults talking about: I get my jersey caught on the door handle and drop my Dolly Mixtures. The bag tears and the sweets make their own way across the pavement and into the gutter. I pick one up, and my mother throws it away.

'Never mind. Maybe they'll have some in next week.'

'Maybe I won't want any next week.'

'Well, I might buy some enamelware instead, then.'

5. GOING SOLO

By now familiar with the High Street and at least some of the terraced streets radiating from the Square, I decided in an unguarded moment to do a little more investigation, but this time on my own. I could reach the latch on Sib's back yard gate and knew how it worked. I'd already been through the entry beyond, and my mother was doing something else. Now seemed as good a time as any.

I soon reached the scene of our various shopping destinations, had been there with my mother, knew the names of the shops and the things they sold. Newbold's Opticians, Oakes' Furniture Stores, Askey's, who couldn't guarantee they'd have finny haddock or plaice but might run to a herring or two, Ball's with its bearded sailor advertising *Senior Service*, occasionally running to *Woodbines* and *Craven A*.

I was quite happy wandering, pressed on regardless of time or the dimly registered fact I shouldn't have been there. I passed Naylor's displays of women's clothes and Bailey's shoe shop fronting the Town Hall without a second glance. Then Keen's, in its alley. Crossing the road was no problem. I'd done it before, and there was nothing on it anyway. I negotiated Parr's, with its tins of paint, Emmanuel's Café, Swettnam's Grocery with its sugar in blue bags and Smith's Cakes with only a few austerity buns on show. I'd reached the Haymarket with scarcely a blink. Here was Maskery's the Jewellers, there Farr's, whose floor to ceiling boxes of screws reached by an ever-present ladder always fascinated me.

I wasn't in the least tired. Nobody asked what I was doing out on my own, and it never occurred to me there was much wrong with my solitary adventure anyway. I got as far as Parr's Chemist where Dr Halpin's prescriptions were collected from a hatch by my mother for my father, whose health wasn't good. That was as far as I knew. I turned back.

The market was a favourite of my mother's and that is where I went now. I threaded my way between stalls and the stallholders who stood less on ceremony than the shop girls, and cheekily engaged local women who gave as good as they got. Curtain material, a trestle table with people drinking cups of tea, unskinned rabbits hanging from hooks above a butcher's head, books and bobbins. It was all there, under a filtered light which made the hall feel oppressive as well as noisily exciting.

I crossed to the Square and the Home and Colonial with its unexpected cash-boxes whizzing through the air. The Square had pace and space. In windows across its width could be glimpsed bikes, cupboards, suits, bottles of spirit and jars of sweets. There was a smell of ale from the Oddfellow's Arms and a display of curiously shaped bottles in the dark window of Hinchco's Chemists. Even at that age, I was aware of a sort of association between bottles, the doctor and the chemist, a sinister trio in some way connected to being ill in bed, and if possible to be avoided.

But I hadn't finished. My grandparents' house was just down the hill, and I might go there. But not yet. The day was bright, and I was enjoying my ramble. I'd do a little more exploring. I'm sure my mum and dad wouldn't mind. This time I'd revisit the streets near grandma's house. In fact Lime Street was as good a place to start as any. The general store was half way down, with its open yard where coal was weighed and bagged. I'd been there before, heard the ping of the bell above the door, leaned against the battered counter surrounded by monochrome wares, smelt the hessian potato sacks propped in a corner almost as dim as that of the street shelter a few steps away.

I took a known entry into Victoria Street, with its windswept playground boundaried by the church wall, hence to Sneyd Street, past the old music hall which looked like a Methodist Church and later became a Salvation Army citadel. Now, Sneyd Street. That was a good street, different. I'd not been there much before. It cut across all those westerly back-to-backs. Here was rubble as well as houses, and willow herb. I took it nevertheless. As far as Nash Peake Street, where grandad's coal man lived. Nash Peake was a notch up in the respectability stakes. I could tell by the low brick walls enclosing a forecourt and a lupin or two, even a line of privets. It was wider, it was going places. The Cottage Hotel and Goldendale Iron Foundry were two of them. And if I carried on walking I'd reach Goldenhill, Goldendale, even Silverdale, those sun-burnished lands of gleaming windows and gleaming people I'd heard the adults speak about. It would be years before I realised what our Victorian city fathers had been up to, and by then I'd placed Paradise Street and Garden Street into the same category. But I didn't care about that now, because I was tired and I wanted to go back.

Then I saw her. My Auntie Ann. Dragging my legs up to the Square as she was coming down. The surprised look on her face didn't really register. I was quite prepared to carry on past. Until she stopped me.

'Bill? What are you doing here by yourself? Where's your mum and dad?'

'They're in the house.'

'You've come all this way from Auntie Sib's on your own?'

'I couldn't buy anything 'cos I ain't got no money.'

'I bet your mum's frantic.' She grasped my hand and marched me towards the High Street. 'Come on, I'll take you home.'

I offered no resistance. I'd had enough of excursions. We met my father in Pinnox Street. He didn't look too pleased. Then he looked relieved, and took my hand.

'I found him up town, wandering.'

He suddenly bent down and jabbed a finger in front of my face. 'Never, ever do that again without me or your mother. Do you understand?

'Yes, dad.'

It wasn't the first of his admonitions, and it wouldn't be the last. But it worked. My peregrinations came to an abrupt end. No more going solo for me.

For a time, anyway.

Cousin Pat and me with Grandma Ridgway, Lime Street, 1944.

6. DOWN THE OVERFLOW

Wandering the narrow brick-floored entries and cobbled alleys was not the only fun. They were fine in their way, but came with rearing walls, half-enders and the odd dead cat. I knew what open spaces looked like. They looked like Tunstall Park, and when coupons weren't available the park was as good a destination as Woolworth's, no matter how enticing the sweets.

My mother and I would make the journey along Station Road (later re-christened The Boulevard by council upgraders in the Fifties), past Barber's Picture Palace, Ryan Hall and the railway station and enter through the high and intricate gates beyond which the central path swept past the park keeper's lodge, the tennis courts and paddling pool.

I never paddled in the pool because it was never filled. And I don't remember tennis matches, though they might well have taken place. Cabbages and austerity potatoes grew where the bowling greens used to be, and it was left to sparse beds of salvia and antirrhinum to oust the greys and khakis of day-to-day life. I suppose they fell under the heading 'boost to civilian morale', the floral equivalent to George Formby, Gracie Fields and Vera Lynn and a thousand miles from the war, whatever that was.

I always made for the playground, still operational then and sandwiched between the path and the pit trains which ran behind a spiked, green fence. The playground was a feast of traps for the unwary. It boasted two shutes, a sand pit, blood-pulsing swing boats, a roundabout, a rocking horse and the sort of dodgy revolving cone which nowadays would have the child abolitionists reaching for their clip-boards. Apart from the occasional grazed knee, nobody seemed to suffer, though both cone, rocking horse and swing-boat were, of course, potentially lethal.

But today I've taken with me to the park an added delight, in the shape of a clockwork car. This had been given to me by my father's friend Frank Danby, who owned a grocer's in the High Street. Frank himself had a *real* car, with spoked wheels and leather seats. Why he'd given me this model I'm not sure, but in my condition any toy was welcome. It had acquired a talismanic aura in my trouser-pocket, to be cherished and admired when there was no longer a space on the revolving cone.

Never a minute passed but my car was subject to a microscopic appraisal. Tyres, wheels, chassis, profile, roof, mudguards and the lights attached to them were examined with the intensity of a Fabergé silversmith. When we eventually left the playground, my car accompanied me down the path to the pools and beyond. It was to be the last trip we made together.

While my mother sat on one of the green slat park benches, some impulse drove me to put my newly-acquired car through its paces. I fumbled it out of my pocket, key still attached, and wound it up until I felt the slight resistance my father had told me meant stop. I'd also been told to hold the drive wheels so that they wouldn't spin until the car was safely grounded.

I placed it firmly on a smooth stretch of path. So intent was I on a good run I'd overlooked the water's proximity and the lake's outfall, a shallow concrete basin which lead to a conduit, hence to the smaller boating lake. The car took off briskly. I followed its progress, and the first pang of trepidation only struck when I realised my new toy was within inches of a watery grave. I reached out for it in a vain effort to bar its further progress. It was too late.

After a moment's indecision, my clockwork car plunged over the edge and into the overflow. I was down on my chest, grubbing helplessly. No use. Still whirring satisfactorily, it vanished from view en route to pond two. No amount of grappling was going to save it. It faded from view, and my pocket had never seemed so empty.

What remains of it is probably still there more than sixty years on, lodged in some inter-lake crevice. I informed my mother of my bereavement, and we walked on by way of consolation, past the boathouse into what was then an untidy patch of wasteland below Little Chell Lane. Then a coal train chugged by, high on the hillside above my head. The sun came out, and in an instant my lost car was just another skein in the weave of time whose luck had run out.

My mother was just as practical. 'Come on, Bill. Let's see if they've got any ice cream left.'

I don't think they had. But it had been a good day in the park, and no minor mishap was going to put me off another visit.

7. A WAR-TIME WEDDING

There was a neighbourliness to my Potteries life, despite adult talk of war and the glimpse of the street shelter through the parlour nets whenever we paid a visit to my grandma's. Anne and Flo's tortoiseshell glasses, Dot's schoolgirl giggles, Gran's bustle and Grandad's longuers - each was a tessera in a mosaic of time and place which comprised my world. My new family was defined by a landscape which provided the narrative for their lives. The horsehair-spilling chaise-longue, cellar mice, brick boiler, back-yard loo and clothes-draped rack, all segments of a grey, but comforting, world.

Or that's how I saw it then. The street itself, in various tones of war-time grey: grey brick walls with cement-grey pointing, soot-grey roofs, blue-grey pavements, a grit-grey road. I saw my family and the local streets as extensions of each other. Victoria Street, Booth Street, George Street, Smith Street, John Street, Queen Street, Piccadilly Street. The Square, Hubank's and the Home and Colonial were *in*, whereas 'th' top end' or 'down Furlong' and the labyrinth centred on Greengates Street and well-heeled Stanley Street somehow fell outside my grandparents' remit - as did the entries which ran through the brick canyons like the veins in a miner's arm.

The Cottage Hotel, at the bottom of Nash Peake Street and close by Goldendale Iron Foundry, was definitely *in*. At least for the duration of the wedding of a distant relative whose name I've forgotten. The full Ridgway clan was there. An upstairs room had been hired and trestles set. It was my first big occasion, and I had no idea what was going on.

I spent much of the time playing with my cousin Pat, and it was more the sight of guests' trousers and shoes under the tables than that of the blushing bride which sticks in my mind. But by degrees the gathering acquired individual forms and faces, and one of these, a fair-haired young man dressed in what I now realise was an RAF uniform, for some reason held my attention.

And not just mine, for there materialised close by a pretty, dark-haired girl who also had him in her sights. Now the draped table cloths which half-concealed strangers' legs and the legs themselves had lost their importance. Something had happened between the dark girl and the blond-haired man. I didn't know what that something was, but I knew a spark had passed between them. I hadn't the words, but signs came before language, and they were the most powerful.

She said something to him. He smiled. She smiled back. He said something, and she smiled again. There was nothing much to it, really, but again there was a lot to it. It was a case of coming to grips with what that *lot* was. He was a man, she a woman. Something was going on, would go on. *What was that something?*

'Are you alright under there?' my mum asked, peering down.

'I'm alright.'

'Why don't you come and sit here. There's an empty chair.'

'I think he's happier on the floor, May,' said a relation I'd never seen before. 'They enjoy poking around under tables at that age.'

Someone put a record on, the music began. The man said something, the girl nodded and smiled and went with him between the trestles to a space in the room. He held her hand and put an arm around her waist and they began to dance, although at that age I didn't really know what a dance was - except they both seemed to be enjoying it.

Snatched glances at trouser level told me something else. Others had noticed, too. There were secretive smiles from the women, whispered comments exchanged, knowing nods given. My observations became more democratic. I was looking at the dancers, then at my relatives, wondering what they were seeing and saying that concerned the black-haired girl in the blue dress and the RAF man in his smart uniform. What was going on that I should know about?

Some records later, some guests departed, the man and woman were still on the floor. But now her head was on his shoulder. They weren't speaking any more, but both seemed more than happy with whatever it was they were happy about. My remaining relatives were now less alert to the situation, but kept in touch through the odd, brief glance, nod and smile. And the gramophone played. And the couple went on dancing.

I didn't say anything to anyone, and in any case my want of years condemned the episode's sexual politics to nothing more than a sub-table stare. For the first time I was witness to the kind of magnetism that would later resurface in Hollywood movies and the posters pasted to the wall of the Ritz. They spent the rest of the night unparted, the other guests irrelevant as shadows.

'Are you still down there? Come and sit here between me and your dad.'

'I think he's tired.'

'Yes, I think it's time we went home.'

What happened to my glamorous couple? What happened to that spark between strangers I witnessed all those years ago at the Cottage Hotel? Did they dance until the guests had left and the room was empty? Did the violins continue to play?

I'll never know, of course. Perhaps it was just a fluke of war. Or maybe, just maybe, they got lucky.

8. THE MINSTREL AND THE BATTLESHIP

My grandparents' house was only slightly more cramped than Sib's. The three of us, my mother, father, and I were relegated to the parlour while Sib, her husband Lou and cousin Pat retained the living room. Likewise, the three of us had the front bedroom overlooking the street, while my aunt and her family used the back room overlooking the yard. As the Allies fought their way up through Italy, and my mother's brother George fought to stay alive while building the Burma railway, I was engaged in a battle for space.

It wasn't easy. My father, pensioned off from the Met and suffering bouts of illness which would dog him for the rest of his life; my uncle and aunt coming home from war work to find the house full of relations - it must have put a strain on things, though it didn't show. And there were amusements - apart from unsanctioned trips up town.

One item which took my fancy had pride of place on the sideboard of Sib's living room. When I was given the opportunity to stray over the border into her territory, I couldn't resist looking at it, then fiddling with it. It was a savings' box in the form of a black minstrel. Only the head and upper body were represented. An arm was attached to a hinge, so that by putting a penny in the outstretched hand and pulling a small lever, the smiling figure could be made to 'swallow' the coin. No doubt my aunt and I would now have to undergo a costly course of racial awareness, the money box itself confiscated for our own good. But I was four, such arcane matters beyond me, and saw it as no more than a fascinating toy. And at that time, toys were in short supply. Even shorter supply since losing Frank Danby's present down the park overflow.

I'd sometimes be given a coin to put in the minstrel's hand. Once regurgitated, I could reuse the penny until I got bored. But on one occasion there was no one about and no coin to hand. Among the junk I'd collected from the backyard was a large washer, and I now decided the minstrel was going to have a change of diet. I offered the washer to his outstretched palm. It didn't fit as neatly as a penny piece, but I did the best I could and pulled the lever.

The washer disappeared half way down the black boy's throat and stuck there. This in turn jammed his arm and the lever which controlled it. I tried in vain to prime the lever. The minstrel's smile never wavered. Perhaps this was a welcome break from routine as far as he was concerned, and he was determined to make the most of it. But how would my aunt react? Maybe I shouldn't have been in that room anyway. Maybe asphyxiation wasn't allowed in the living room.

I had to think laterally. I decided the best course was to remove the washer, return it to my pocket, and go and look at a picture book in the parlour. I thrust my fingers down the figure's mouth until I could feel the washer and tried to yank it out. That's when my uncle came in. Nothing much was said. He went into the kitchen and returned with a screwdriver and a pair of pliers. The minstrel was taken to the table and tipped to face the window light. The indignity of swallowing both washer and screwdriver had no effect on his inherent good humour. I watched my uncle prize, lever and fiddle and after a moment the washer was eased towards the waiting pliers, and out onto the table top.

'You'd better have it back,' Lou said. 'It won't eat anything but pennies.'

'I didn't have none.'

'Well, don't feed him washers again or he'll get all jammed up.' He returned the figure to the sideboard. 'It'll soon be your birthday.'

'Will it?'

'Well, don't put anything down his mouth or you might not get a birthday present if you hurt him.'

I had a hazy idea of threat, entangled with hazier ideas of what a birthday was. But Lou was a sanguine man, not given to scolding, and my birthday produced an unexpected gift from him. It was heavy and came in aluminium paint: a battleship. I was presented with it in the living room, which for my birthday had become a rare, communal space.

It was hard to come to terms with my new acquisition. It was bulky and heavy, and no superstructure was evident - though at the time I didn't know ships had one. The colour was the most attractive thing. The fact battleships weren't painted bright silver, the puzzle as to where the paint had come from in those years of deprivation - not to mention the body, which comprised hull-shaped pieces of wood of diminishing sizes glued together - didn't much figure on my birthday.

Although my boat looked unlike any of the graceful model yachts I'd seen on the small lake in Tunstall Park, I saw this as a likely destination. Alas, it never got there. Such was its bulk, the journey up hill would have been a step too far, even with my mother's help. And she wasn't helping. My boat was relegated to the already cramped parlour, where it took pride of place on the window sill.

I'm sure there were other forgotten items of greater interest than the minstrel boy and the chunk of ship-shaped wood presented to me on my fourth birthday in that Pinnox Street living room. Perhaps the minstrel boy is still out there somewhere, receptive as ever to a diet of new coins. Or washers.

9. STARTING SCHOOL

A sense of events drawing to a close settled on the house. Adult conversations seemed guardedly optimistic, with 'It'll soon be over' and 'Not long now' interspersed with a new word - school. Though it was explained to me what school was, that I'd soon be going and there was nothing to be done about it, I was still apprehensive.

My age was the clinching factor. 'You'll soon be five, but Miss Featherstone says you can start after Christmas.' Miss Featherstone? Who was that? Maybe she couldn't be all bad if she had a feather in her name. But what was a headmistress? What was it for? An uncertainty had sneaked into my life, which Bing and the Andrews Sisters couldn't dispel even with a fully charged accumulator. *Don't fence Me In* took on a poignancy Bing hadn't intended, sung from the confines of our parlour, and did nothing to lighten my load. But now school, until then only loosely associated with crayons and Miss Featherstone, became a reality fleshed out in bricks, mortar and a name: St Mary's.

'Have you done behind your ears?'

'Yes, I done 'em.'

'Hurry up or you'll be late.'

'How far is it?'

'Just up the road. Pull your socks up.'

'My garter just broke.'

St Mary's was in Lascelles Street, a narrow thoroughfare off High Street leading to the grid of terraces of which my grandparents' was one. There were no houses in Lascelles Street. Only a jumble of packing sheds and out-of-true walls penned between a brewery and Sneyd Street. The school seemed ill-placed alongside its industrial neighbours, though both school and the buildings to either side were equally nondescript. A cobbled snicket skirted the school and the emergency water tank behind it. The yard, hemmed in by the school on one side and a warehouse on the other, was separated from the pavement by railings and from a wall at the rear by a section of corrugated roofing which served as storage for those items which wouldn't easily fit into the school itself - the maypole, for instance, and people like me, who didn't think they'd fit in either.

Abandoned at the gate, I took a first hesitant step into the playground and froze. The children I'd played with in Pinnox Street were few: I'd no idea they could now exist in such numbers. Across the yard, girls in pixie hats skipped to rhymes of which I was ignorant, while boys in ill-patched jerseys ran in hip-slapping imitation of Hop Along Cassidy. The damp-shadowed bricks echoed to the screams of chasing figures, figures being chased and figures being solitary, all clad in the dull garb of austerity which seemed to cling to the school and its surroundings.

One, two, three a-lairy, my ball's down the dairy, Don't forget to give it to Mary, not to Charlie Chaplin

The girls turned the rope, the rope beat the brick. A grey-haired woman emerged from the shelter, whistle in hand. By the time she blew it, I had moved warily among the throng. They slowed the moment they heard the blast. 'Ethel Wright, put your rope in your pocket, now. Hurry up, Tommy, stand still. Stop fidgeting. Now, line up. Make a straight line. One behind the other. I'm waiting for you all to stop talking. Completely still. Can I hear a pin drop? Can I? Alright, Mary, you may lead the way.'

I tagged on, neither knowing who I was tagging on to nor where I was being led. I approached the entrance door with increased misgivings. 'Who's that?' I plucked up courage to mutter. 'Is it Mrs Feathstone?'

'It's Miss Riley. Don't you know who Miss Riley is?'

'I only come today for the first time.'

'He doesn't even know who Miss Riley is. Why do you speak funny?'

'I come up from London 'cos of the war. Where's Mrs Featherstone?'

Giggles. 'It's *Miss* Feathstone, not *Mrs*. He can't even talk right.'

Miss Riley was now guarding the door as coats were hung in the corridor outside. 'Quietly, now, quietly. Go in very quietly and take you seat.'

Take my seat where? Everybody knew what they were doing except me.

'Please, Miss Riley, this boy says he's new and he hasn't got a seat.'

'I know all about it, Lucy. Go and sit down while I sort it out. Are you William?'

'My mum calls me Billy sometimes, sometimes she calls me Bill.'

'Haven't you got another name?'

'I don't know.'

'Well, I think it's William Ridgway, don't you?'

'That's my dad's name.'

'And it's your name too. Now, there's a spare seat over by the window. Go and sit down in it while I put your name in the register. Can you do that?'

Conspicuous amid veterans who'd started the previous September, I pulled down the hinged seat and shuffled mournfully behind an initial-scarred lid. As I traced one of the letters with my finger, I wondered if Miss Riley would teach me how to write on the desk too.

10. LEARNING TO READ

In the hullabaloo of my first days at St Mary's, I'd forgotten about Miss Featherstone. But she was not to be so easily relegated, for now she appeared at our classroom door, a small, neat woman in wire-rimmed spectacles and an unadorned face which seemed both kind and censorious. Having just got used to Miss Riley's motherly tortoiseshells and ample proportions, the discrepancy between them put me on the alert. Even then, a hazy notion of a 'system' was beginning to impress itself upon me. This sense of hierarchy was ravelled up in codes of body language, deference and assertion, and it taught me that teachers were on different levels of whatever structure prevailed. And that, in St Mary's at least, the diminutive Miss Featherstone was calling the shots.

But Miss Riley was our reference point, the provider of cardboard games and cardboard alphabets, counters, abacuses, toy cars and paint; of frequent admonition and daily praise, cloistered with the rest of us behind the water-tank while the Allies fought their way to Berlin. It was to Miss Riley I applied to 'leave the room' when I couldn't wait any longer. And to her I offered my Ministry of Food Dried Milk tin when she'd been favoured by the Americans to dole out chocolate powder to her pupils.

However, school wasn't all chocolate powder. The tyranny of the unfamiliar soon gave way to the tyranny of routine. School was for doing things in, and Miss Riley was the orchestrator of their daily rhythm, moving seamlessly between worlds of which I'd previously known nothing. No sooner had we taken our place alongside Milly Molly Mandy than we were whisked to the Front, our renditions of jaunty war-time songs conducted by Miss Riley's blackboard ruler:

Run, rabbit, run, rabbit, run, run, run.
Here comes the farmer with his gun, gun, gun
He'll get by, without his rabbit pie - so run, rabbit, run, rabbit,
Run! Run! Run!

'You weren't all singing. Let's go over the words again. Put your heart into it and we'll see if we can raise the roof!'

Words and letters. Chalked on the easel as we made the sounds in unison, sang them out, copied them in crayon onto sugar paper, laid them in cut-outs on the desk top, checked and re-checked them until we could call the sound from Miss Riley's flash cards with the assurance of a corporal assembling his Bren gun. From such beginnings the penny began to drop. At some point, Miss Riley's runic scratches coalesced into written words, then spoken words with meaning attached. I began to think up more elaborate words - containing my evolving horde of letter-groupings, those *ars* and *ees* which were starting to unleash their secrets.

These unapprehended words now intruded on vans and buses, in shops and on them, into my father's paper and onto my grandparents' range. We said them when we sang *All things bright and beautiful*. They appeared on boards and desks, even on a plaque set into the school wall: *'To the Glory of God in the Faith of Jesus Christ. This stone was laid by the Rt Hon Edward George Perry Littlejohn, Lord Hatherton, July 5th 1910.'* This was language in unfamiliar form, and it didn't get any easier at the park gate, where *'In Memory of Thomas Nash Peake by his children, 1904'* dented my growing confidence.

Maybe I was less cut out for this reading lark than I believed. In any case, I'd only taken the first stumbling steps towards the pitfalls of print before someone said the war was over. A strange excitement rippled from school to street and even gained a toe hold in our parlour. Radio reprises of Gracie Field's *Sing as we Go* and George Formby's *Bless 'em All* punctuated any lingering sense of disbelief. The maypole was dragged out, Miss Riley's Acme Thunderer trilled across the backs and my parents' conversation turned to knees-ups and dos.

Novel events lay in store. Bonfires were lit along the shard-strewn patches of waste, the sky was full of blinking stars and drifting woodsmoke. Around the blaze, chiaroscuro figures sang and prodded the embers, the trains rumbled over the viaduct, the buses under the trains. Was it the following week I was hauled to another party, this time in Lime Street, in my crisply-ironed shirt and polished shoes? This was a more formal affair, with trestles stretching from the shelter to the crossroads and plenty of tea poured from double-handed enamel pots. And all the street were there, a final glimpse - apart from the Coronation celebrations eight years later - into the kind of communities which had survived into the Fifties.

Not long after, someone called Mr Attlee ousted a Mr Churchill in something called the General Election, which pleased my dad but did nothing to impress me. I was too busy adding to my newly discovered skills. Rupert Bear hid in Bradwell Wood and Korky the cat roamed the entries. I met them both, along with a lot of fairly strange people who'd recently come to light on the ill-understood pages of some book or other.

The war might have ended, but I couldn't help feeling Miss Riley and I still had things to do. Reading was just one of them.

11. A WASP IN MY MOUTH

The bonfire smoke had hardly faded when my mother announced she was going hop-picking in Kent and I was going too, together with a pal who lived near my aunt's house. She'd written to her sister in London, who was to join us there with Pauline, my cousin. My father was to stay in Tunstall, where he'd managed to get work red-leading hoppers for a local firm.

'What are hops, mum?'
'They make beer out of them.'
'Where's Kent. Mum?'
'Near London.'
'Why can't we stay here?'
'Because we're going hop picking in Kent.'
'What are hops, mum?'
'Hurry up or you'll be late for school.'

I hadn't been on a train since my evacuation three years earlier, and anything to do with trains was alright by me. My mother, my friend and I watched Tunstall, then Burslem slide by from our vantage point on the top deck of a PMT bus. I thought I remembered Stoke Station, and the compartment we shared was familiar enough, with its seaside pictures under the racks and the window-opening leather belt inviting us to fiddle with it - which we did. The only thing different was the absence of soldiers. Then the trains had been full of soldiers. Now there were civilians in suits and hats instead.

From Euston we caught a bus to Charing Cross - or was it Victoria? Another train, another journey. We were flagging. A wash of brown streets ran past the window, then trees and fields.

'When will we get there?'
'Not long now. We'll soon be in Sidcup. The farmer will give us a lift in his lorry.'
'Where's Sidcup?'
'In Kent. Where we go to pick hops.'
'What's a lorry?'
My pal: 'My uncle's got a lorry.'
'Where's Kent, mum?

It was getting dark by the time we left the train, and the truck was waiting by the picket-fence, the farmer at the wheel. A group of fellow hop-pickers who'd also been waiting clambered into the open back and sat alongside us on the sacking. Most were from the East End, and the jokes flew as we jolted down the lanes to our billets. We shared ours with my mother's sister and my cousin. There was a smell of hay and wood smoke, a last glimpse of hedgerows under a dusky sky, something rustling somewhere, and I slept.

We awoke to a chrome-bright morning and voices. The smell of sizzling bacon drifted through the open door and we were up and on the move. My pal from Pinnox Street, older than me, was first off the mark. He'd already discovered the farmer's tractor and levered himself into the seat. There was room for two (nearly) and I climbed up beside him. We took it in turns to 'drive', twisting the steering wheel this way and that until the approaching farmer, who we hadn't noticed, collared me.

'Get off that bloody tractor before I give you a back-hander!'

'We was just havin' a bit o' fun, mister,' ventured my pal.

'Well go and have some fun helping to pick hops. That'll give you something useful to do 'stead o' messing about up there.'

My mother and Ivy seemed to be enjoying the country life, pulling the hops off their nets and dropping them into sacks to be carried away by women from other billets with their children in tow. Voices sounded across the fields, talk of the ended war, the latest film, who slept well, who badly. And the hours passed in bright sunshine and the work stopped for lunch.

They laughed and chatted with the excited camaraderie of those who'd lived through the bombing and escaped the bombs, though they all had tales to tell and horrors to forget. The countryside was magical, the space free and the sounds they heard no longer sent them scurrying to the shelter. Now I was in a different place, far away from Tunstall and St Mary's, the voices strange yet familiar, with a warmth and vivacity I hadn't been used to.

But my elegy didn't last, because my belly beckoned. Jam was the answer. Jam sandwiches all around. My mother handed me mine, and I took a first healthy bite. Almost straight away, I realised something was wrong. A sharp pain had attacked the inside of my mouth. I gave another chew, and the pain increased. Suddenly, I spit the bread and jam over the grass.

'Maybe the crust was sharp, May,' my aunt said, clutching at straws.

'Open your mouth, let's have a look.' said my mum. I complied. 'Come and look at this, Ivy. His mouth's all red.'

'D'you think it was the crust, then?'

'There was hardly any crust on any of 'em. I wonder what you did?'

Perhaps it was my Tunstall friend whose morbid desire to inspect the ejected contents of my mouth clinched the case.

'Look, Mrs Ridgway, it's a wasp.'

'Look, Ivy, he's been chewing a wasp'

'I bet that hurt. Is it still hurting?'

'It hurts a bit.... is there anything else to eat?'

An unusual incident, but hardly ground-breaking, and I'm surprised it's stood the test of years. But it has, and lingers with glow-worms at dusk, the wheeling of birds across a nightfall sky, the sound of crickets and the soft plock of ball against bat on the edge of memory.

I think I knew then what war was, and that it was finally over.

12. DISTANT VOICES

My mother's brother, Harry, died when I was two, before the first of my journeys to Tunstall as an evacuee. I only know him from photographs and my mother's description. I don't remember my mother's grief, though she did grieve then and on subsequent occasions when some small incident triggered the memory of those buried war-time years.

Harry had joined the navy before the war broke out, and served as a mechanic on cruisers patrolling the Mediterranean. His scrap book, with its well-composed photographs showing refugees from the Spanish Civil War, the poverty of the Greek Islands, a camel ride near Cairo, enlivened by the descriptions given by this young, adventurous seaman seemed remote from the gathering storm.

When war was declared, he found himself aboard the cruiser *Cornwall*, a 10,000 ton ship on patrol in the Indian Ocean. By the end of 1941 the Japanese had entered the war, and rapidly turned their sights on the Philippines. During the ensuing battles, the Indian Ocean became a graveyard for Allied ships.

HMS Cornwall and her sister ship *HMS Dorsetshire* were detached from the convoy of vessels patrolling the seas between Ceylon (Sri Lanka) and the Sunda Straits to escort the Hermes, an aircraft carrier, to Colombo for repairs. They were on action stations the moment they resumed patrol.

Harry worked in the engine room. His job was to maintain the Cornwall's fresh water system, which produced drinkable water from the sea through a system of evaporation. That's what he was doing when the Japanese planes left their aircraft carrier and, with a cargo of 500lb bombs, came out of the sun towards the ship. It was Easter Sunday, April 5th, 1942, when the first bombs struck.

The order was given to abandon the ship, which was sinking fast. Most of the crew were able to make it to the upper deck, but those in the engine room and boiler room had no chance. It took no longer than 12 minutes for the Cornwall to go down. Harry was among the 198 lost. That night he came to my mother in a dream and told her he wouldn't see her again.

The 650 survivors were picked up by the cruiser *Enterprise* and the destroyers *Panther* and *Paladin*. The following day, Lord Haw-Haw told those listening to the wireless that the Cornwall had been lost. But my mother already knew about her brother. I had my red pedal car and my train book. Harry had been killed and the future, if there was a future, was mine.

Harry's brother George was also a reservist, but he'd chosen the army. While Miss Riley was teaching me my letters, George was in the thick of it. The day before Harry was killed, George was embarked in a tramp ship for Saigon, a prisoner of the Japanese Army. Five days later he witnessed the execution of two comrades who'd attempted to escape their prison camp in Hanoi. By December 1942, deaths from dysentery, inadequate medical supplies and shortage of food were commonplace.

By the summer of 1943, he knew what lay in store. He knew he was going to be put to work on the Burma Railway - the troops knew it as the Death Railway. Three years earlier, on leave, he'd taken his young son Kenny to Regent's Park Zoo for a day's outing. Now George was in the jungles of South-East Asia, making a diary on any scrap that came to hand:

'Working conditions appalling. Hours from dawn to dusk. Japs driving us all the time until we are physically exhausted. No hospitals, no medical supplies. Dependant on the river for all water, which has to be boiled.

'Much dysentery. Deep mud everywhere, always wet. Many deaths from Cholera. Such cruelty by Japs. Like a nightmare, pouring with rain the whole time, little food. Two men went mad, two killed by falling off bridge, one lost in jungle.

'No sleep because of mosquitoes and sand flies. Marching all the following day barefoot through jungle. Passed many corpses. Work on building big bridge (River Kwai). Fetch timber from jungle in rain and mud, climb mountains for timber barefoot, causing me much suffering and a few bashings. Contacted malaria and dysentery, and collapsed. Had three weeks in hospital. (a bamboo hut) Hardly any medicine, but a tin of condensed milk. Rest did me good. Lost a lot of weight. All along the line, thousands of Allied POWs dying....'

Miraculously, George survived. I remember going to Liverpool docks with my parents to greet him. It was Monday 15th October, 1945, and I'd been given the day off school. Two months later he was back in his old job at Glaxo Laboratories in Greenford, where he worked until his death in 1970.

George and Harry went unheard amid the hubbub of my subsequent Potteries life. There is much to do, and listening to distant voices may be seen as an indulgence. But thrown stones cast ripples, and Harry might have been amused that sixty years after his death on *HMS Cornwall* we found his daughter.

For Harry had been a married man when the war broke out, with a daughter, June. In the confusion during the final stages of the war, my mother lost contact with his widow, Rose. From time to time she would wonder, aloud, what had happened to her, if she had re-married, where she was.

My sister's foray into family history provided an unexpected answer. Rose subsequently married a Canadian, and emigrated with June to Canada in the early Fifties. As I was writing the last of my articles for *The Way We Were*, my sister tracked them down.

Now there's another voice, distant in miles rather than years, but still part of the upheaval that thrust us into Sib's cramped parlour, hoisted me aboard squaddie-packed steam trains and imprinted my prized book with shelter-mud.

Mum's brother, Harry, newly married to Rose. Harry was lost when his ship was bombed in the War.
Rose later re-married and emigrated to Canada.

2. KITES, DENS AND DUMPS

We moved from our temporary parlour in Pinnox Street into one of the new council houses in 1946. Our estate at Chell Heath was then under construction, an emblem of a confident future with a bath and interior loo as well as gardens front and back. Built on the site of former coal workings, with a dump almost on the doorstep and Whitfield Colliery down the road, it nevertheless went some way towards providing the post-war homes 'fit for heroes' Lloyd George had promised more than thirty years earlier.

I was almost seven when we moved in, though I've forgotten our arrival and how we made it. I do, however, remember the feeling of space. Space to play with my Bayko kit and Hornby train inside; space to chase Polly or Phoenix, the labouring coal trains making their daily journeys to and from Whitfield, through the shale-strewn field opposite. I'd left the close-knit terraces behind and seemed set for a new direction - even though a bus from Sprink Bank would take me back to Tunstall in five minutes for a 1d each way.

My dad had gone to teacher training college under the emergency scheme and we'd got our own home at last. Things were looking up.

Whose turn to wind? Playing trains with Mike, 1950.

Chapters

1. Moving Home
2. Wood Stain and Liver Salts
3. A Tricky Situation
4. More Dumps and Dens
5. Looping the Loop
6. Crossing the Rubicon
7. Lost in the Garden
8. Friends and Strangers
9. Ike and the Mafioso
10. Quick March!
11. Polly
12. A Close Call

1. MOVING HOME

In odd moments at Sib's, my father's spirits lifted and he'd break into song. This was a rare event, and probably as surprising to him as the rest of us. My mother had no such qualms. Protected by an East End chirpiness, into her psychological repertoire had crept supportive aphorisms learnt from childhood which she'd repeat when things took a turn for the worse. 'Don't let it get you down', 'You have to take the rough with the smooth', 'Every cloud has a silver lining' defined her view of the world, interspersed with snatches of Ivor Novello, Jerome Kern and Sigmund Romberg.

She'd break unselfconsciously into *The Desert Song*, notwithstanding her brother Bill was still fighting in one. If a change of location was called for, the Saharan wastes could be substituted for an English lane, where she'd 'gather lilacs in the spring again', or, failing that, the deck of *Showboat,* where, both Magnolia and Gaylord, she'd conclude with *Only Make Believe*, a theme that fitted well with her situation.

The letter telling my father we'd been offered a council house at Chell Heath precipitated one such mood change, and to celebrate he broke into a duet with my mother. His renderings of *Only a Rose* and *Overhead the Moon is Gleaming* were so out of keeping with his usual gloom it was difficult to decide if this was a step in the right direction or he'd finally taken leave of his senses.

In one of those sweltering days which seemed to last the whole summer, my mother struggled with my brother's push chair and me up Little Chell Lane to view our new home, Number 54, Sprink Bank Road. The road itself was then no more than a rutted track.

'It ain't half hot,' she'd exclaim, her native cockney later diluted with the passing years. 'I don't think it's that much further. I should have brought me 'at.'

We found ourselves in a far-flung post of Empire. The corporation tip, the defunct clay quarries, the remnants of farm walls, some collapsed into croaking ponds, surely hadn't escaped her notice. But the offer of a council house outweighed such inconveniences, and she bumped the push-chair along a makeshift pavement under the relentless sun.

'I could do with a drink. A nice glass of lemonade would go down a treat.'

The tip was a grey plain speckled with paper, glinting cans and broken bottles. A corporation cart trundled towards the waste; across the ash-field a figure laboured with a rake. Just past the tip, over the lip of the hill, lay our new house. The roof was on, but it lacked windows and criss-cross struts had been nailed across the door frame. Wheel imprinted marl lapped the walls amid a detritus of old buckets, battens and clay-encrusted shale. In the valley half a mile away, Whitfield Colliery stack spiked the sky.

We'd left the terraces behind. Here the air was untroubled by smuts and the rumble of Tunstall traffic. Here were wide vistas and familiar sounds borne on the currents.

'Hark at them coal trains. Can you hear them, Michael?'

'Are they the same as down Tunstall Park?' I asked.

'I expect so. They're coming from the pit. We can't get inside the house yet. I don't think it'll take long to finish off, though. Not at this rate I don't.'

It looked far from complete to me, but my mother had moved on to livestock. 'Oo, Michael, look at them cows!'

A herd had strayed from the fields at Bradeley to rummage amid the footings. But my brother was already asleep, and we turned around.

'Come on, Bill, we'll go back to Tunstall, see if we can get an ice cream from the place in the park. Wait till I tell your dad about the house. He won't half be pleased.'

On our way back we passed a heap of builders' lime. On the ground beside it lay a dead shrew. The shrews in Pinnox Street, if there were any, had kept themselves to themselves. This was the first wild animal I'd seen, and seemed to add a further twist to what was already, to me, an exotic destination. Moving house had now moved up a notch in the excitement stakes, together with trains to watch and the promise of a room to bath in - although I hadn't seen it yet. Yet of the moving itself, which must have happened towards the end of that 1946 summer, I have no memory.

What few things we possessed could have been loaded into a small van. All I remember of Sib's parlour is a couch and easy chairs, both the worse for wear, and an eiderdown in which could still be felt the debris of London bombing - though, mysteriously, there were no holes. But it must have been a relief to leave her parlour floor, hemmed in by walls and upholstery and thwarting my early attempts to amuse myself through lack of space.

In our new home, space abounded. Days passed before I came to terms with the vast expanse of Walpamur, the steel-framed windows, the half-open staircase with its landing and newel posts, the built-in wardrobes large enough to hide not only my brother and me, but lions and witches too.

My parents now began to fill their new acres with second-hand furniture.

Iron-framed beds appeared, together with a folding table. The couch and easy chairs made their appearance. Other items from an earlier time were allocated corners from which they never strayed for the next fifty years: an Edwardian wicker chair which had once belonged to my mother's mother; a lacquered side table, purchased on my parents' wedding in 1937, when art-deco was all the rage; a couple of spindle-legged kitchen chairs.

Over the weeks other items appeared. A marble clock in the shape of a Greek temple came and went. A piano arrived and left. A boiler came unexpectedly to light in a corner of the kitchen. Other accessories found a permanent home: a complementary set of prints showing a woodland in May, azure with bluebells, and in autumn, bronze with leaves, hung from the picture rail. And above the mantelpiece, a pretty girl, proud her absent Tommy was doing his bit for Kitchener, smiled wistfully through the gloaming.

The print had once belonged to my maternal grandmother, and bore the caption *Absence Cannot Hearts Divide*. Until 2005, when the house - my father had purchased it under Thatcher's 'right to buy' scheme - was cleared ready for sale, the picture remained in its place, the auburn-haired girl for ever awaiting her unreturned lover, much as Madame Butterfly had waited in vain for Pinkerton.

Thus we settled into our new home, unaware that within a few months we'd be digging our way out through snow drifts in one of the worst winters in a generation.

2. WOOD STAIN AND WATER BEETLES

I can't remember the point when home became home, just as I've forgotten the upheaval of moving from my aunt's front room to the new council house Mr Attlee had kindly provided for us in Sprink Bank Road. There was the parlour overlooking the main road and railway viaduct, then an entire house with a red-tiled roof and unmade gardens. One morphed into the other with neither regret nor joy of anticipation. A cord had been cut. I was adrift in strange lands far from the comforting rows of Tunstall back-to-backs.

But the image was quick to fade. Moving had also awakened some atavistic nesting instinct in my father, whose forays into home-making had never properly been realised. He seemed to have taken on board the song of the moment, *Now is the Hour,* and decided there was no time to waste.

A good starting point was the floor, and he was anxious to stamp his identity on it. His next visit to town produced a large tin of wood stain, which he'd bought from Parr's, a decorator's near Tunstall Market Square. His ambition to enhance the floors throughout the house was greeted by my mother with casual disbelief, while I was delegated to stir the tin.

His dedication was remarkable, since he'd always prided himself on being disinterested in décor of any kind. In any case, those preferring a more subdued palette would have found themselves at odds with his taste in stains. The understated tones of beech, pine and light oak were anathema to him. The word was ebony, and the few purchases he made in the furniture line throughout my childhood conformed to this general rule. He tested an area of boards in the small bedroom to start with. Pleased with the result, nothing could hold him back. Before winter set in, the floors throughout the house had taken on the carbonised look which was his stock in trade. Moreover, he'd painted around what carpets we had, going for economy and aesthetics at one fell swoop.

His first flush of enthusiasm waned. Whatever energy he still had would now be held in reserve until the coming spring, when I'd help him convert our rubble-strewn land into a garden of sorts. But the intervening winter, with drifts blocking the front door and days spent in, gave me time to ponder my parents' eccentricities. I didn't get very far at the time, and it was only much later I came to the conclusion that my father's predilection for dark wood stains was mirrored in his taste for strong foods.

My mother had a sweet tooth, but my father's taste was for the savoury, the acidic and the bitter. My mother ate at the table - bread and butter pudding, bubble and squeak and bacon fat unresented by a digestive system in full working order into her nineties. On the other hand, my father had his fireside chair and ate soused herring from a plate on his knee. The only exception was on Sundays, when, after the *Billy Cotton Band Show*, he'd join us at the table for a roast.

Gorgonzola was up there with Bovril, vinegar-marinaded fish, Worthington E and Worcester Sauce, and he suffered for it. A packet of Rennies was on constant stand-by, as was a tin of Andrew's Liver Salts, which he took with such frequency I came to regard it as an aperitif. Before he knocked it back, there was the same ritualistic approach to its preparation as there was later to Alka Seltza. The ratio of powder to water was scrupulously observed, the effervescence peaking at the moment of swallow.

I was engaged in observations of my own, and these family idiosyncrasies eventually took on the hue of normality, at least as far as I was concerned. I came to lump my father's taste in bitter food and his liking for dark wood stains together, part of an overriding character trait I was still coming to terms with and associated in my mind with moving to our new home and settling to a new life.

The spring of 1947 thawed the field through which the coal trains plodded, turning paths into quagmires. This didn't put us off making the front garden, however. A range of tools appeared; a fork minus a tine, an edging spade with part of the handle missing. Clods of various thickness and none were hauled from the backs, the grass spade-flattened without finesse into a sort of lawn. Birch saplings were planted, privet cuttings scrounged, rocks excavated and placed in interesting positions which neither looked like, nor felt like a rockery.

I was seven, and my days were bright with possibilities. The songs of approaching summer cascaded from a mare's tail sky, accompanied me on my daily journeys to school and danced among the billowing sheets. No land was safer than my land, no road wider, no field airier. The coal-trains' comforting chunter, the pit-hopper's distant clang and the roar of the Port Vale crowd crowded my idle moments and defined my world.

Hidden in the tufts I discovered my first brown-speckled skylark's eggs. I watched the parent bird sprinkle its joy across the sky, scatter its song over the banks of shale, offer it to me and to anyone else who was listening. I crossed the footbridge which straddled the mineral line and found a reedy pond. You didn't have to wait long to see the first amphibian swim through the peaty water. I'd seen pictures of newts at school, but those were drawn and these were real, as were the electric blue damselflies which sparked among the reeds. And if I waited long enough I might catch a glimpse of a silver water beetle diving in the shallows.

The pool, the shale-strewn cutting through which the railway ran, the grey-green waste framed by cinder-coloured banks and mysterious depressions, defined my new world. It was a joyous world of breeze-tousled grass and china skies. My aunt's parlour lay discarded on the edge of memory, her minstrel money box forgotten, the viaduct erased. I had other fish to fry, and I saw no reason why I shouldn't fry them.

3. A TRICKY SITUATION

The shadow of austerity still lingered after the war, and some mitigated its effects by supplementing their shopping with home grown produce. Back gardens were dug and manured ready for vegetables, and the more adventurous even experimented with fruit growing. Not everyone submitted to such outbursts of enthusiasm, but the ones who did were rewarded with plentiful supplies of lettuce and potatoes, and, if they were lucky, strawberries without the cream.

Our back garden never seemed to acquire the status of the front. Though it didn't become a dump - the rag and bone man was always on hand to remove saleable junk - it remained in limbo, part yard, part willow-herb. No attempt was made to tame it, and apart from laying a path under the clothes line, it lay neglected until the late Sixties, when the advent of electric mowers made rudimentary maintenance possible without too much effort.

Vegetable growing demanded commitment and expertise, and my dad wasn't the gardening type. But it occurred to him that our dietary needs could be as easily met through the egg cup as the salad bowl. He decided to keep chickens. That way he'd be doing his bit for the family and keeping the grass down at the same time.

I don't think a conventional hen run was ever laid out. The chickens, which had materialised one day while I was at school, had the back 'garden' to themselves, and were happily pecking about in it. I had scant knowledge of poultry. I knew that hens laid eggs and that was as far as it went. But even I could spot the taller, more powerfully built stranger in their midst.

'Your father's bought a cock, and it's taken a liking to the line post. How am I going to hang out my washing with that thing brooding over me?'

Realising it was the subject of discussion, the clock obligingly flew to the top of the post, where it spent the next half hour keeping an eye on things.

The year passed. We had our eggs, but the cock had become more assertive. Now the hens were no longer the sole object of its amorous intentions. My mother's back also proved worthy of desire, and after a final attempt to hang out the washing with the bird's talons embedded in her peg-bag, she gave my father an ultimatum.

'You'll have to do something about that bird.'
'What d'you have in mind?'

"If it was up to me I'd have it put down.'

'What about the hens?'

'It's not the hens I'm worried about, it's the cock. Either sell it or get rid of it.'

'Getting rid' of a bird the size of the Graf Spey was no mean feat, especially for a man of my father's disposition, but in the end he was forced to concede defeat. Moreover, *he'd* do the deed. He'd been led to believe the job would be easy and painless as far as both he and the cock were concerned. He fixed the following Saturday as the end of chanticleer's dive-bombing routine. Peace would once more reign in the house and out of it. After the mission had been accomplished, he'd sell the hens and buy eggs from the shop, like everyone else.

The day arrived. He'd already decided execution was best confined to the outhouse, away from the prying eyes of neighbours who might be alerted to the bird's plight if things got out of hand. He'd acquired the pallid look of a soldier destined for the Front. The cock, however, had no such qualms, and was perched on a weed-heap shouting the odds.

My father closed the back door behind him and went to face the enemy. Taking a scoop of seed from a bag, he set about laying a trail which would lead the cock into the outhouse, where it could be speedily dispatched. After a temporary altercation with the hens who'd gathered to enjoy the feast, he managed to entice it in. The door was quickly shut, pinning the combatants between a tool cupboard and the back wall.

I have to rely on my father's account of what happened next. An expert in the pub had informed him that a humane death could be guaranteed by wringing the cock's neck, followed by a swift upward jerk. The move was practised, using an empty stout bottle, until perfect. A hasty death was assured. The man would even cart off the carcass free.

In practice, this was easier said than done. The cock had other plans, escape being uppermost, and it had managed to reach the relative safety of a high shelf before my father could lay a hand on it. In the ensuing struggle, the bird was brought down to earth and this time my father did, indeed, manage the wringing part.

The cock lay prone. Congratulating himself on a speedy resolution, and considering it unnecessary to complete the upward jerk he'd practised earlier, my father tentatively eased the door open to give us the good news. So it was something of a surprise to find chanticleer had returned from the dead and flown up to the tool cupboard, where it began to pour scorn on my father's lack of success in a series of squawks audible throughout the estate. Again the door was shut.

Desperate measures were now called for. Oblivious to the instructions he'd been given in the pub, he hunted desperately for anything that would do the trick. On the shelf lay an old tennis racket, and he clung to it like a drowning sailor to a life-raft. We waited in the yard. Eventually my father's swearing and the cock's crowing ceased. He'd effected his *coup de grace*.

The man now leaving the shed was a pale imitation of the poultry dispenser who, half an hour before, had strode inside to do the business. My mother helped him to the bench.

'It'll be the last time I do anything like that,' he managed at last. 'I think I'll go for a drink.'

Though after this episode we kept the occasional pet, poultry was never again on the agenda. The hens went the following week, the back garden reasserted itself and my mother made a new peg bag.

4. MORE DUMPS AND DENS

I was an early convert to dens, and before the Forties were up I'd helped to construct quite a few of them. The tip was a useful starting point for any materials needed, and our dens were usually built on a rim of rough grass which overlooked it to avoid the problems of haulage.

There was no shortage of refuse, disgorged by a fleet of wagons whose daily cargoes were borne under a curved steel canopy, first to the weigh bridge, then to the dump face. The tip itself lay in the bowl of an old clay quarry which extended from High Lane to what became Sprink Bank Road. Each day brought a new tally of broken dolls, cracked china, rotting window frames, decapitated ceramic figures, cast-off struts, worn linoleum, used cans, smashed bottles and half-enders to the site.

By the early Fifties, the area had been filled in, but that would be a few years hence. Now, great expectations were afoot as we scouted for treasures amid new faces arising from the old cinder beds. Perhaps my nose was insensitive to the unpleasant smells this wasteland produced, for I have no memory of them, even though a westerly breeze would have carried any stench up to the 'tin-tack' houses which had been built almost on the lip of the quarry - not to mention our own house, not much further off. In any case, we were more alert to the attentions of the 'dump men', who didn't take happily to scroungers, than to unpleasant odours.

My three or four newly-acquired friends were older than I, and knew a thing or two about dens. At eight or thereabouts, I was just the monkey, tolerated as long as I played my part in dragging our haul up the slope after the dump men had knocked off for the day.

In the end I entered into the spirit of the thing. A den was not something to be taken lightly. It was a serious business, even though no one knew why they were doing it. There was a mystery to it which kept us occupied until the newly-installed street lights began to flicker and the haze of early evening crept upwards. I wasn't even sure why the word 'den' came to be associated with the precarious structures in which we invested so much of our energy. Once the thing was complete - assuming it hadn't collapsed during the night - there was nothing we could do but sit in it.

I didn't worry about that at the time. Building it was the thing, its purpose irrelevant. First, spades were 'procured' and a few yards of turf and soil removed.

That took most of the day, the inevitable shirker retiring for an early lunch with the excuse 'my mother'll belt me if I get in late but I'll let you use my spade.'

Into the ad-hoc dimensions were introduced our scavenged trophies - old doors, window frames, planking, boarding, threadbare carpets, cardboard and rope. A collective decision was sought how best to utilise our windfall. After a process of deliberation, which usually included doubts cast on each other's architectural vision (and, on occasions, his parentage), a sort of inverted coracle was produced.

Each oddment was roped to the next to create a structure which, though falling short of building regulations in force at the time, was worth risking. This was covered in boards, doors, carpets, canvas and, if sufficiently robust, by the turf we'd excavated earlier. More adventurous models included a hole for smoke when the inevitable fire was lit. The goal was an unhealthy gloom unimpeded by daylight, and if possible a roof which would keep out the worst of the weather. Spare lino, if we had any, would be used to cover the floor. Some considered this a luxury bordering on the effete.

A box or two supplied the seating arrangements and if only one box was available, Reg, 'the boss', would commandeer it. From time to time a real chair would turn up at the dump, and I'd ingratiate myself with Reg by hauling it back so he could sit on it, my reward being the use of his box, which by then would be smeared in marl.

Merely sitting in our den could get boring, however. One or the other would feel disaffected, and when the fire got going and its smoke refused to drift through the hole in the roof as 'the boss' had promised, the member would decide now was as good a time as any to hoof it home. But Reg was nobody's fool. He'd thought up ways of keeping us up to the mark. Now a solemn meeting was convened and a secret password issued, known only to him and the initiated. In future, you had to remember to whisper your password to Reg on the other side of the opening before gaining admittance. Our den was thus the forerunner of the sort of menacingly democratic social inclusion policy New Labour would later embrace.

'Password?'
'I forgot it.'
'Can't hear. Speak up.'
'I said I forgot it.'
'Louder.'
'I can't remember it.'
'Don't shout, I'm not deaf. No password, no entry. Get off home.'
'I've just remembered. It's *Battleship*.'
'You made it up. That's not your password.'
'I know it's got ship in somewhere.'
'Go home.'
'Please, Reg, all the others are in. Come on, Reg, let's come in - '
'Clear off.'
'Right, you can stick your password. I wouldn't be seen dead in your tatty den anyway. I wouldn't come in if you paid me. It stinks.' A kick would be aimed at what passed for the door. 'Call that a fire? I've seen more fire on a match.'

The hapless victim would slink home, forced to suffer the rest of the afternoon in the snug comfort of a dry house, rather than enjoy the virally suspect interior of Reg's den. And I, who'd remembered my password, could sit with a charred potato and reflect on this further example of the hierarchical nature of human societies - Miss Featherstone's and Miss Riley's place in the school pecking order not yet forgotten. Yet though 'the boss', could micro-manage the inmates of his den with the ease of a fur-trapper controlling his huskies, he couldn't stop the roof from leaking, and the first shower was accompanied by a rush for the exit and home.

Sixty years on, all that survives of the tip is the frame of the weigh bridge, its attendant building and a section of the pre-war railings which once protected the site. The tip itself has long been levelled off and seeded to provide football pitches. Now trees are growing where we made our dens, gave our passwords, lit fires from damp wood and watched the trundling wagons discharge their cargo.

5. LOOPING THE LOOP

Other interests vied with dens and dumps. By this time my brother and I had acquired a Hornby train set. In the box we discovered a dozen sections of curved rail which, clipped together, formed a circular track. Before our green clockwork shunter and its three trucks could be sent on a journey, the spring had to be fully wound. Turning the key was a mark of prestige as well as a potential source of conflict. At first my brother and I shared the winding with restrained bonhomie. Such equity soon wore thin, however. Before many nights had passed, the engine was removed from the tracks and used as a bargaining chip to secure the next turn, the next anything, until complacency set in and other distractions beckoned.

One of these was my Meccano set. I was fortunate enough to have sole custody, since my brother wasn't interested. My introduction into basic engineering has always been a mystery, for I've shown little inclination in this direction since. My beginner's pack kept me happy once the structures shown in the accompanying booklet had been completed and I could get to work on oddities of my own. Choosing from drilled steel ribs, triangles and rectangles of various sizes, together with pulleys, wheels, shafts and even twine, I was able to create a range of spectacular items of dubious function.

This theme continued with my Bayko kit, where the idea was to build a house using rods of various lengths set into a drilled base, and small plastic 'brick' panels slotted between the rods for walls. My Bayko came with a red roof and red and white walls. Both windows and doors were green, and it too kept me busily engaged when rain threatened.

But these were inside activities, and did nothing to allay my passion for the great outdoors. It wasn't only den building that drew me through the front door. Sledges in winter and trolleys in summer honed my practical skills, though the end products were nothing to brag about, and I put kite making into the same category. The template for constructing a kite seemed to have been hard-wired into my brain before birth, and not only mine. The estate was full of hopeful fliers whose designs never deviated from a shared blueprint.

First it was necessary to find some lightweight wooden struts - garden canes would do. A 'T' cross was bound together using twine or tape, the extremities joined in a similar way to form the framework. Pinned, tacked or glued to this would be a piece of fabric - an old pillow case, for example - cut to shape, its edges wrapped around the canes. If fabric wasn't available, sized tracing paper would suffice until the trial run, when it usually got ripped and the project shelved for another day.

Stability of sorts was supplied by the tail. A string some four feet long was fixed to the lower apex. Along the string's length were tied rag bows at intervals of about a foot. All that was left was to find a bobbin of twine, tie one end to the intersection and set off for the backs.

The Wright Brothers couldn't have been more elated to see their first plane airborne, and it was usually touch and go whether my kitchen-table kite took off. Luck, season and a stiff breeze played their part as, careering down the runnels of grey waste, I tugged at the twine and felt the hesitant upward snatch which heralded success. If I'd got it right, the next billow would sweep my collection of canes and cotton into the heavens. If my luck *really* held, I could race alongside Polly or Phoenix and outrun the clanking trucks as they moved into the cutting, pulling my kite after me.

I was not the only one who saw that these breeze-tousled tablelands represented freedom. Casting my eye left and right, other kites soared, their handlers dotted across the plain as far away as Fegg Hayes and Chell Green Avenue. Some had taken their pastime more seriously than I, experimenting with colour, form, and tail-length. In some cases emblems had been added to the fabric - a dragon's head, a sword dripping blood, an eagle, a wolf and other logos etched in crayon or painted in the outhouse on a wet afternoon. The most adventurous had even gone in for a box kite, which was a notch up in kitemanship and out of the range of the rest of us.

This kind of kite was more a statement about the owner than the thing itself, and both he and it could expect to soar to Olympian heights in terms of street cred if all went well on the day. You probably had to refer to a plan of some sort to make it, the intricate cane structure worked out in Proustian detail beforehand and a foray into the household fabric drawer essential when seeking that treasured table-cloth which, when cut to shape, would provide optimum lift.

From these early beginnings a pair of hollow boxes would be formed, separated from each other by lengths of cane. It was larger and bulkier than the simple affairs most of us put together, and judging by what I saw harder to get airborne. But skilled practitioners were never put off, and when the wind was in the right direction the box kite eclipsed both our own inferior offerings and the Whitfield Colliery chimney in the valley below.

I wasn't envious. Over the next few summers, I learnt to make my makeshift collection of rag and cane dive, swoop and loop the loop. I flew it to the end of its tether and mine, dive bombed it into the long grass, repaired it, raced with it and fought to keep it under control when the wind blew up and threatened to snatch it from my grasp.

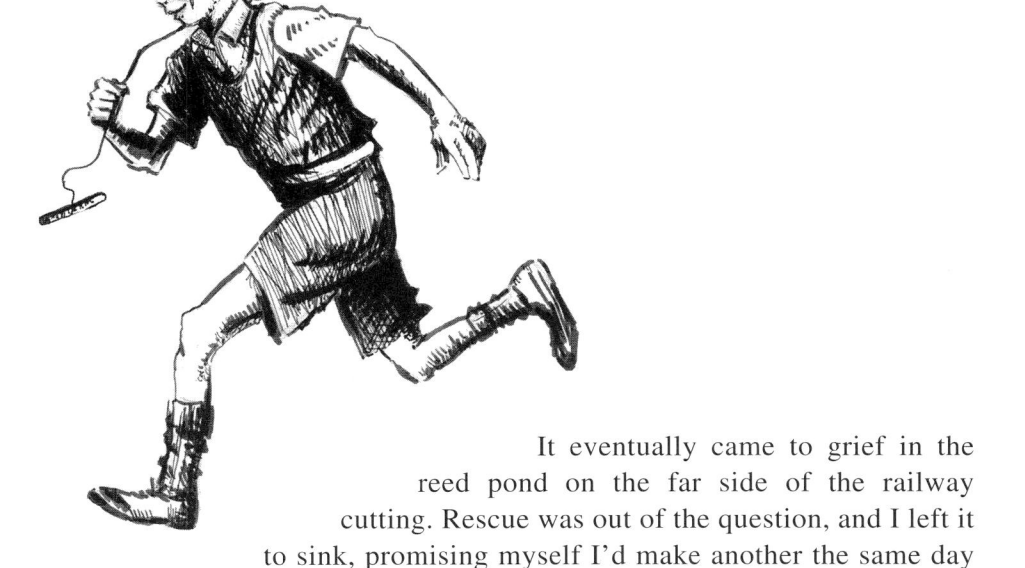

It eventually came to grief in the reed pond on the far side of the railway cutting. Rescue was out of the question, and I left it to sink, promising myself I'd make another the same day or the next. I don't think I ever did.

Perhaps I'd moved back to dens again.

6. CROSSING THE RUBICON

For a time I'd set an arbitrary boundary at the wasteland and mineral line on my doorstep. But now a languid April had turned the winter drifts into melt water, and it was then, in that spring of 1947, that I made up my mind to investigate further. On various excursions I explored the western Rubicon of High Lane and the eastern provinces which lay to the far side of Chell Heath Road. I even ventured into the foothills of Fegg Hayes, a procedure made hazardous by tribal hostilities which flared up at key times of the year - notably before November 5th, when competition for bonfire wood was at its height, and in winter, when snowball fights raged.

I was seven, and the world was full of intrigue - particularly an area of coarse grass at the junction of High Lane and Little Chell Lane where the remnants of old farm walls lay scattered across a pocket of waterlogged clay which would soon be home to a colony of croaking toads. The site sloped upwards to the face of a disused quarry beneath which a scattering of wind-lopped trees stood in clouds of wood sorrel. The formation on the opposite side of the road, with its hummocks and grassy hills, was equally mysterious. Standing on the top you could see the glinting tip and the first of the houses in Sprink Bank Road from a different and fascinating perspective.

This western side of my estate had the mark of the quarryman on it, but no such undulations were visible along Chell Heath Road to the east. This area, too, had suffered from extensive mineral working, but the goal here had been coal, not clay. One pit brooded over the site: Chatterley Whitfield Colliery. Though this part of the Chell Heath estate had been built amid a previous century's debris, it was the pyramid of dirt which lay just beyond which drew the eye, a towering heap of slate-grey spoil which the waste hopper climbed relentlessly. The release of its cargo of dross was accompanied by a clang audible throughout the estate, the scree of shale and stone bowling in flurries of dust down the sheer sides of the heap to form lesser heaps at its base.

Pockets of farmland had survived the encroachment, and here cows still plucked at the grass. And although the houses had now reached the Biddulph Valley Line, the children of the newly-arrived hordes hadn't yet fished out Banky Brook's minnows or culled the rats which made their nests in the banks of the stream.

A farm was still working on Chell Heath Road then, and I recall passing the byres one evening as the cows were being milked. After the war, the road was nothing more than a hawthorn-hedged lane linking the old miners' village of Chell Heath with similar communities at Bradeley and Fegg Hayes. Most of these latter terraces survive at the time of writing - unlike the old village of Chell Heath, which was bulldozed away in the Fifties. My father frequented its pub. When last orders were called he transferred his allegiance down the road to the Knave of Clubs, a show-piece building erected for the benefit of the occupants of the new houses which now surrounded it. A few years hence, when he was too tired to go out, I'd be delegated to pick up two pints of mild and one of bitter from the off-licence and cart the bottles home in the saddle-bag of my bike.

The Knave was not the only local feature of post-war planning. The organic growth which had given English rural villages their character and made them desirable to live in was not an option where the rapid delivery of bricks and mortar was concerned. Like other estates laid out in the late Forties, Chell Heath had been hamstrung by a Ministry of Works sameness of design, which has now been addressed to some extent by the addition of porches and other distinctive features. Yet it is difficult to fault the planners' intentions, for alongside the dull plod of conformity came tree-lined roads, a then state-of-the-art school and shops.

The newly-planted saplings were frequently vandalised during my childhood, but the council doggedly replanted and eventually won the day. The shops in the early years were less fortunate. They changed hands frequently, unlike their counterparts in town which had been in the same family for generations. Although it was then hoped these amenities would provide the focus for a new and vibrant community, recent arrivals would complain they'd rather be in Tunstall or Burslem where the action was.

Of course, all this was lost on me then. Shops, pub, pit and sapling-lined road, larks rising from the wastes and ponds croaking their invitations - these described and defined the contours of my days. No hour passed unutilised and as yet complications had no place in the scheme of things.

The Knave survives much as it was then, but the shops have changed to other uses. Chell Heath Junior School has been demolished, its generous precincts sold off for private housing. The spoil heap at Whitfield Colliery has been lowered, firmed, sculpted and grassed, and those climbing to the top are rewarded with a far reaching view of the surrounding estate and countryside.

The pit buildings at its base remain as a testament to the quest for coal, and to the energy produced and harnessed by the colliery in full spate.

The Biddulph Valley Railway track bed is now a pleasant greenway. The mineral line's tunnel and cutting have been filled in, its route through the old wastes remembered only by a dwindling band whose simple pleasures lay in finding a four-egger, skittering down runnels of hardened slurry on a length of ply or feeling the pleasurable tug of a home-made kite. The stone-strewn pond at the top of Little Chell Lane has been municipally grassed over, the old quarry face hidden, the clouds of wood-sorrel buried beneath the bulldozed earth.

Together with my solo journey around Tunstall three years before, those twin Rubicons of High Lane and Chell Heath Road would be the first of many I'd cross in the years to come. They were my navigator's chart and the orienteer of untroubled hours.

Our new house at Chell Heath.
My brother looks apprehensive as I pose for the shot. 1949.

7. LOST IN THE GARDEN

Just before we moved to Chell Heath, my father and his friend Frank Danby had visited Burden Park, Bolton Wanderers' ground, to watch the FA Cup-tie with Stoke City. The perimeter fence collapsed, leaving thirty three dead. My father and Frank had anticipated the tragedy, and made their way to safety at the back of the ground before the barriers went down. Even so, the episode badly effected my father, particularly coming so soon after the war, and at odd times he would speak to us about it.

Though nothing as catastrophic happened thereafter, other minor incidents did occur which would unsettle him for a time. One was killing the cock, which took him some days to get over. The other was the loss of his wedding ring, although the outcome here was more favourable.

Soon after the cock had been dispatched, the back garden reverted to its former state. This time willow herb was in competition with the dock and thistle which had established itself in vigorous patches of couch grass. Even the slabbed area laid down when the house was built was partly submerged beneath weeds and brambles, and nettles had intruded along the path used by my mother to hang out the washing. Not to be outdone, hawthorn and blackthorn shoots were beginning to sprout. The bolder specimens were already in leaf when my father decided it was time to act.

This was a new phase. Cocks were out, horticulture in. My dad was going to become a gardener and grow some fruit and veg. This was an unexpected venture, something that would simultaneously add carbohydrates to the plate and convert our weed-bed into something useful. It was all systems go from the moment the scorched-handled edging spade and the fork with a prong missing were taken from the outhouse. My mother had bought him a leather jerkin for his birthday and now he donned it to look the part. First the weeds had to be got rid of, then the garden dug over. He began right away.

It was hard work. Larger stones were manhandled to one pile at the back; dock, grass and thistle to another. Brambles were dug out and added to the heap, along with embryo trees and a range of grasses comprehensive enough to make botanist's eyes water. I helped or hindered as he dug, each pile growing satisfactorily under threatening clouds.

The first spots were enough to curtail his enthusiasm and we disappeared inside for a cup of tea. It was there, surveying his handiwork through the window, that he suddenly realised he'd lost it. He asked my mother if she'd picked it up but she hadn't. He put down his undrained mug and began lifting cushions, then rugs. We could hear him barging about upstairs in the bedrooms, then downstairs in the hall.

He came crestfallen into the living room. 'I remember now, I put it on the sill while I was shaving. But I was wearing it before I went out. I must have dropped it in the garden.'

At that time my father had lost weight, and during his exertions in the garden his wedding ring, already loose, must have fallen off. My mother had given him the ring on their marriage in 1937. He hardly ever took it off, wore it always when he went out. For the first time in almost a decade he and it were no longer an item.

'I'll have to find it,' he said. 'It'll be in the garden somewhere.'

'I can't see you finding it now, not in that lot,' put in my mother by way of consolation.

But he was now oblivious to the spitting rain. His loss had made him recklessly methodical, and he began anew, starting in the corner and digging over the spadeful he'd turned over two hours earlier. The earth was broken up further with the fork, each section examined minutely before moving on. The spots of rain grew heavier, the clouds more menacing. Now a rake was produced, the twice-dug section reduced to the sort of fine tilth sought by competent plantsmen everywhere. No matter what the outcome of his labours on the ring front, at least he'd be in line for some reasonable carrots and potatoes in due course.

But by now his excursion into fruit and vegetables had been put on the back burner. Finding his wedding ring had become not only a priority, but an obsession. Neither rain nor lumbago stood a chance against his obstinacy. He dug, turned, forked and raked as if his life depended upon it, moving steadfastly down the garden section by section.

The light was beginning to fade. His leather jerkin glistened with rain, his forehead with sweat. He was on the case. Nothing could put him off, least of all my mother and I, marvelling at this continuous burst of activity from behind the nets. Half an hour later, he'd almost reached the limit of his previous digging. The twin evils of dusk and desperation were beginning to settle on both him and the garden.

'He'll never find it now. It's probably dropped down a crack,' my mother said, injecting a note of optimism into the proceedings. 'It'll be dark soon.'

Dad turned the final spit and stood back. The ring had disappeared without trace. It could be anywhere. He returned his tools to the outhouse, came back in and poured a beer into the straight pint glass he reserved for moments of remorse or high stress. He said, 'Well, that's it, then - ' and retired to bed not long after.

At first light he was at it again. Spade, rake, fork and fingers were employed in this, his final putsch. No lump was left to chance, no item of clay-encrusted debris remained unsifted. The result was the same. My mother came out and handed him some tea.

'Well, that's it then. It's gone.'

He drank mournfully on the touchline, leaning on the handle of his rake. Mum eyed the mounds of turned earth with disinterest. Then she said: 'What's that?'

'What?'

'That, over there. I thought I saw something glinting.'

The place located, my father bounded over to it like a bloodhound on the scent. He reached down into a cleft of heavy loam, gave a rare shout of triumph and held the ring aloft.

'You'd better have it made smaller,' my mother said, 'or it'll be off again.'

I'm not sure that happened. I think we had cabbage a lot that year, but the gardening phase wasn't going to last. As for the ring, it never came off again. And finding it was, of course, the excuse for a later celebratory trip to the local.

8. FRIENDS AND STRANGERS

The well-intentioned council estates which sprang up after the war signalled the end of the sort of community life which had been taken for granted by those living in the back-to-backs. The spaciousness of the new houses precluded the sort of intimacy which closer living dictated, and an increase in wealth meant neighbours were less reliant on each other. Chell Heath, where I lived, was 'away from things'. Those who'd moved there were no longer necessarily employed by the handful of pot banks where generations of workers had been drawn from the same families living in the same streets and everyone knew the other's business.

The recent upheavals of war had brought together not only the working man, but the dispossessed professional, the insolvent, the white-collar worker whose life had been disrupted by hostilities and the occasional foreigner. Hard times had gusted them into any harbour they could find, and all groups were represented in the local streets.

Even so, we got to know our neighbours well enough to be neighbourly. Mrs Edmondson, who was prepared to act as midwife to my mother had not the ambulance arrived in time, lived opposite, next door to the Hands and across from the Woollams. Phoebe Moreton was our immediate neighbour, with the Dudley brothers a few doors down and the Golding and Bossons families, each of whom had a child who went on to grammar school and entered the professions, nearby.

Mrs Edmondson was very much a woman of the time. Dependable and good-natured, she wouldn't have been out of place pouring tea from a two-handled Naafi pot, or officiating at Girl Guides' Jamborees. Her husband was one of the Potteries' contingent of horse-mounted police. Mr Woollam, his London-born wife and their family shared a well-kept house which backed on to the old colliery waste, as did the Goldings' house further down.

A diverse collection of other characters populated the estate. Eccentrics shared the streets with half-wild mongrels, torn-eared toms, school-leaver miners with the airs of family men, sit-up-and-beg bikers, helmetless motorcyclists (who were frequently chased by, and lashed out at, the dogs), chain-smoking twitchers, a cart-trundling fruit and veg man and housewives laden with bags.

I foraged in the fields with the Dudley brothers and from time to time brought someone home from school for a jam sandwich and a game of shotties. I also made a friend in nearby Chell Green Avenue, a road of pre-war semis free of mongrels but with garages, some of which contained a Morris or a Hillman. This was far up in the respectability stakes, despite the fact its unadopted road was virtually impassable in winter.

This new mate was therefore a sign of prestige. I was invited with others to his house for a birthday party and fancies. After we'd eaten, we were blindfolded, and presented with a cardboard tail, which we were to pin to a paper donkey. The one nearest the mark won a small gift wrapped in crepe paper. Other games followed, my friend's father relishing his role as Master of Ceremonies, the mother passing around the lemonade and petits fours, the same thing no doubt going on in countless other semis at party time in those innocent days. After tea, we were given paper and crayons and invited to draw a picture. The father would judge whose was best. My friend drew a bus against the sunset, I suspect because his father was involved in transport in some way. My crayon broke while I was drawing a tree, and shortly after I went home with my gift - everyone seemed to have one - in the pocket of my burberry.

Hostilities sometimes flared on the estate. There was the odd fight, and occasional internecine squabbles rippled between the youths of Chell Heath and those of the Fegg Hayes estate on the other side of the mineral line. Then there were *implied* hostilities, which I couldn't grasp.

'They're Catholics, they are.'

'What's that?'

'Catholics. *You know.*'

Was I missing out on something? Those whispered asides, the tail-end of centuries of pointless prejudice, even came to the fore in our own house later, when a girl I was going out with turned out to have Irish forebears.

'Nothing can come of it,' my father had pronounced solemnly. 'Nothing can come of it, she's a *Catholic.*'

His uncompromising stance was at odds with his liberal outlook. I could never understand what the fuss was about, and he probably couldn't understand why he made it. But even he had to admit Catholics weren't *foreigners*. Friends, Catholics, foreigners - at the time, the words were nothing more than ill-understood concepts. Then, in the last year of the Forties, concept hardened into reality when for the first time I saw two *real* foreigners walking down Sprink Bank Road.

I knew they were foreigners, but I didn't know how I knew. There was nothing strikingly different about them. The man, stocky, short-legged and broad shouldered; the woman, an attractive brunette with an aquiline nose. They walked in detached silence, oblivious to the street and to each other. I saw them frequently from then on, plying the same route at the same time. Where had these strangers come from? Where had they been, where were they going?

In later years they sometimes popped unbidden into my mind, and with the benefit of hindsight I wondered if they'd fled pre-war Germany, or one of the other Axis countries - the girl might have been Jewish.

But I was nine, and nine year olds don't ponder for long. The estate and its life teemed about me, and friends and strangers were part of the pulse of things. I didn't then know that conclusions had to be reached, so I came to none. The important thing was living for the day, its twenty four hours unwasted.

My brother Mike (2nd left) and me (right)
with the Dudley brothers. 1950.

9. IKE AND THE MAFIOSO

My father had taken to Pittshill Workingmen's Club in a big way. Children were allowed in, and youngsters like my five-year-old brother, not to mention me, four years older, had no trouble getting through the door. After a certain amount of lubrication, my father would 'do a turn', which involved mounting the stage and singing one of the popular songs of his youth. My mother took no part in the proceedings, and by ten o'clock the atmosphere in the room had mellowed sufficiently for any lapses in pitch and lyric to be overlooked.

These Friday treats seemed to stretch well into those dusky Forties nights, and bed time beckoned before last drinks were called. But there was one occasion when the party continued after closing time and accompanied us all the way to Sprink Bank Road.

My father, a gregarious man made more so by a visit to the club, had invited his cronies back, and Ike was one of them. Ike was the Master of Ceremonies at the Club. His job was to keep the audience under control when 'turns' were being performed by pinging a bell and, if that didn't work, by stopping the show and bawling 'Order!' at the audience.

Now we were making our way back in jocular mood, Ike leading, the other patrons bringing up the rear armed with bottles of bitter and bags of stout. My brother was walking in his sleep, and part way along Chell Green Avenue, my dad hoisted him on his shoulders. No doubt the dozen or so of us making our way past those curtain-twitching semis came in for some flak. And with good cause, as the inhabitants were now treated to a member's falsetto interpretation of 'Yes, we have no bananas' and Ike's well-oiled confirmation: 'We have no bananas today'.

A voice rang out from the shadows: 'Why don't you lot bugger off home and get to bed?'

'Roll out the barrel -' Ike countered, unfazed.

'We'll have a barrel of fun -' joined in falsetto man, 'but not here we won't.'

Home was just around the corner. My brother was taken to bed while I was allowed a rare late night to observe the frivolities. Someone came up with the idea of democratising the ale ration by inviting everyone to pour his bottle into the kitchen boiler. This was a large, galvanised cylinder containing an element and a tap. The idea was that during the proceedings, anyone who wanted a drink could turn on the tap and decant a pint into one of my father's glasses. Why this unique system of inebriation was put into action I don't know, and the partakers didn't care.

The songs went on, the jokes flew. I had a last glimpse of Ike, who'd somehow managed to squeeze onto my brother's toy tricycle and was pedalling furiously around the room, before I went to bed. By next morning, last night's debris had been cleared away and my mother was sitting at the table reading the Express.

'Your father's in bed with a hangover.' She went back to her paper. 'What're you up to today?'

'I might go and see if anyone wants to play.'

'That's right. It's a nice day, go and get some air in your lungs.'

Last night's party wasn't mentioned, but the week-end had only just begun. Now a different sort of party was gathering on the street. There was some commotion, a few shouts. I stood at the gate and watched the group climb the hill. The youths formed a tight-knit scrum, one or the other shouting the odds to anyone within earshot before relapsing into mock fights and banter. At intervals individuals would break away from the ranks and pull ahead, or hang back. The mob drew nearer and fragmented. Now there were two groups, one trailing the other, with plenty of ribald exchanges between the various members.

I knew now what all the fuss was about, and my suspicions were confirmed as they turned into the cul-de-sac which led to the old colliery wastes. It was then I caught sight of two figures in the midst of the melee who didn't seem to fit. They might have been in their early thirties, family men perhaps. One had a coat draped over his shoulders, like a Hollywood Mafioso. The other wore a jacket. Both were surrounded by a supportive clan of well-wishers and back-slappers. There was going to be a fight.

Neither man looked keen to enter the fray, but, egged on by the tribe, would have lost face had he not gone through with it. Now they were on the edge of the tableland and making for the 'bowl', a venue for cyclists who'd wheel-smoothed its sides and come to grief more than once at its base.

One or two locals were looking on from the end of the cul-de-sac. In the bowl the crowd gathered. The mafioso slipped off his coat and squared up to the other man, who'd taken off his jacket. Their backers brayed and brayed louder as the fight began.

The Queensberry rules were lost on the belligerents slugging it out in the backs. A lot of chasing around and out-manoeuvring was done, a lot of dodging and weaving. Few blows actually landed. The crowd roared, the fighters lunged.

Encouragements fell upon deaf ears, but honour had to be done. One man went down, the other followed. They made it to their feet and squared up.

'Oh, ah?'

'Ah.'

'Oh, ah?'

'Ah.'

I went back home and whipped a top along the path. Not long after, the victor was escorted from the scene by his team of minders - some of whom had earlier been acclaiming the hardness of his adversary. An apologist for the loser maintained: 'He would've won except he was wearing his ring on the wrong finger and couldn't hit straight.'

I never did discover what the fight had been about. Nor did I see another one in the bowl, which reverted to its former use as a 'doffer' for cyclists and a graveyard for bikes. The dispute settled, the following week would see them both at work and friends again.

Not unlike Ike, who'd glare once more at his audience through thick-rimmed glasses, ring his bell and call for order.

10. QUICK MARCH!

By 1947 I was taking my lunch at home, for this was the year I moved from St Mary's Infants' to the Primary School at Chell. Over the previous year I'd continued to make the journey to Tunstall by bus - a penny each way - not a particularly hazardous feat in those days of freedom, and to have a lunch-time sandwich at my grandparents' house nearby. Now change was afoot.

There were the usual pangs of trepidation, but this time I was a more seasoned veteran. Yet there were worries. I'd grown used to St Mary's. It was intimate and intimately situated in its tightly-knit cluster of buildings. I'd grown, the school had shrunk, and both Miss Riley and I had bustled comfortably along within it.

St Mary's wore carpet slippers, but Chell wore steel-tipped clogs. It stood in splendid isolation, a cranky old man garbed in black who seemed to welcome new-comers with a gnarled hand swishing a metaphorical cane. Here I had to face new teachers - and this time they wore trousers.

Schoolmasters, rather than mistresses, were not the only idiosyncrasy of this new phase. Segregation reared its head for the first time. The beat of skipping ropes now came from the girls' side of the wall, and boys were left to their own devices. These included horseplay, hoarse play, shotties, slide making and conkers in season, and brief, punished fights throughout the year. These activities took place in a playground hidden from the road by the school, and there was a sense that both school and inmates were somehow removed from the pulse of local life.

The High Lane traffic rumbled by unnoticed, and the panting colliery engines fell silent as they plunged through a shale cutting into the tunnel nearby.

I was no longer a stranger to regimen, but this time there were echoes of the parade ground thrown in. Whereas Miss Riley had brought play-time to a halt with a trill of her whistle, Mr Salmon, the whistle-blower at Chell, felt it his duty to lick us into shape the moment we arrived. Bespectacled and lame in one leg, he'd give a long blast, followed by marching orders in which the mild-mannered teacher morphed into a bulge-eyed Sergeant Major.

'Keep still. Stop moving.' Whistle on standby. 'Dobson, you were talking!'
'I wasn't, sir.'
'Don't answer me back, boy. Stand by the wall. Put your hands on your head. The rest of you stay still. Now. Get ready....wait for it....Right - TURN.'

We turned indecisively towards various compass points as we struggled to come to terms with Mr Salmon's order.

'That was extremely poorly done. We'll start again. No whispering. I SAID NO WHISPERING. One arm's length apart. Now. Hold up your right hand. I said your RIGHT hand, Hughes, not your left. Right, that's right and this is left' He demonstrated. 'You should know that by now. We'll try again. Right - TURN!'

By this time we'd figured out the door into school lay roughly in the direction of Mr Salmon's outstretched arm. Some of us had already begun the journey.

'STOP! I only said turn, not move. Get back in your lines and wait for the order. Stand to attention. Arms by your side. Perfectly still. Wait for the order.. Wait for it....'

Not unlike Ike ringing for quiet in the club next door or the Bond villain whose mastiffs fall on a salver of raw meat only on hearing a belated click of his fingers, Mr Salmon made the most of this military approach to child welfare, eyeing his charges under the brim of his trilby with the rapt attention of a hungry kestrel. Eventually a veil of silence settled on the yard. A bus rumbled by on the other side of the school. The girls had already left their playground, and we heard the door shut behind them. There came the distant chuffing of a train starting out from Pittshill Station. The columns waited in silence.

'Line at a time, starting with you. Steady.... steady. Forward - MARCH!'

The previously straggling infantry now welded into a fighting unit, we made our way briskly towards the annex where the entrance was situated. Mr Salmon was by this time fully engaged in a private world of military manoeuvres. The tilt of his trilby suggested he could hear bugles in Tunstall Park and was preparing to outflank us if things didn't go according to plan.

It was usually rain that signalled the end of his reverie. The mantle fell, and he reverted to Mr Mild.

'Come on, lads, it's beginning to spot. Hurry up and get inside.'

The arrow-straight line which had been Mr Salmon's pride and joy needed no further encouragement, and broke ranks as the troops scurried to get under cover. But the teacher, well-placed at the front, elbowed his charges out of the way and got there first.

Mr Salmon was sometimes accompanied in his playground routine by a Mr Page. Mr Page was younger and more reticent than his colleague. Whether he was taking it all onboard as a sort of training exercise or simply wore an accommodating face because he needed a job, I don't know. I can only remember Mr Salmon and Mr Page in the context of us lining up in the playground ready to come into school. I have no memory of either of them teaching me.

That job was left to Mr Hanford, one of those gaunt Forties men you'd see waiting at the bus stop in trilby and gaberdine and who seemed to have suffered from post war deprivations more than most. And like the situation at St Mary's, where Miss Featherstone was the boss and Miss Riley knew it, at Chell Mr Quinton ruled the roost and our class-teacher let him get on with it.

Mr Salmon relished his role as sergeant major and I learnt the drill off by heart. Two years later, when I changed schools again, I departed from Chell with a sound sense of orientation. I could line up, straighten up, shut up and march in with the assurance of a seasoned squaddie on the parade ground. It could get tricky in winter when the yard was icy or wet, but then the rules were waived and Mr Salmon and his buddy Mr Page were first through the door.

Those morning and afternoon rituals were the nearest I got to the demands of call-up, which was curtailed just before my eighteenth birthday.

11. POLLY

There were other things to contend with, apart from drills. Chell Primary was older than St Mary's for a start. It hadn't changed much since the last years of the 19th century, when the first scholars filed through the door. It was not only out-of-date. Parts of it were out-of-bounds too, and the only way we knew girls were about was the sound of their voices behind the wall at play-time and the swish of their ropes against the brick. St Mary's was cosily nestled in a short, dusty street no one ever seemed to walk down. Chell was immune to all the weather could throw at it, and occupied a windy height within a stone's throw of the old workhouse.

My classroom was a high-raftered cube of dingy plaster. Cords from the tall windows hung to shoulder height and were looped around cleats fixed to the wall. On rare occasions Mr Hanford, who'd been retitled Polly Rubberneck before my time, would open the windows. Like a tar at the rigging of a four-master, this involved an unfurling of the cord which was nautical in its complexity.

Rows of hinged desks faced a board and easel which had no doubt occupied the same space since the old School Board requisitioned them sixty years before. An assortment of cupboards, dulled to the same ochre shade, had their allotted place around the walls and held the few books deemed essential for our enlightenment. A lacquered world map took its place alongside the easel, the red of Empire still the dominating colour even as Britannia herself was sinking beneath the waves.

A partly-glazed door led into a corridor serving the other classrooms and Headmaster Quinton's office. We were fortunate enough to lack the benefit of a National Curriculum, and as a result grew up functionally literate and mature. Unimpeded by help from central government, Polly was able to enliven his class with enthusiasms of his own, the seldom-used stick a cost-effective alternative to counselling should the need arise. He was a man of his time, the daily schema tailored to his own requirements and a blind eye turned to timetable constraints.

Neither one of the wise-cracking brigade nor despot, he steered a mild mid-course, did the best he could and took the bus home, untroubled by what the next day might bring. He worked at a steady pace, the sleeve of his tweed jacket riding up his wrist as he chalked copperplate tables, measures and verses on the board as we looked on in silence.

He faced a daily sea of patched jerseys, ripped pullovers, hand-me-down jackets, running noses and shorn heads.

'This week it's the six times table. The six times table. It's on the board. Hands up all those who can't see it. Right, one six is six. Two sixes are twelve. What are three sixties? Anybody?'

'Sir! Sir!' Eager hands flew up, their owners thrusting out their chests and craning their neck in the hope they'd be the chosen one.

'Don't call out. It's not a race. Three sixes?'

'Sir! Sir! Me, sir!'

'What have I told you about calling out? Well, Jones?'

'Please, sir, eighteen, sir.'

A dissident muttering would arise; growls of sedition could be heard.

'Stop that whispering. Sit up straight. That's better. If you want to ask a question, raise your hand.'

Polly would turn briefly back to the board. Fascinated by his jutting larynx, which developed a life of its own as he was speaking, I was quelled into submission in time for the sing-song chants which followed. These were orchestrated by his sleeve-escaping wrist as he pin-pointed the line to be read and later, when the board's contents had been erased, by his ruler as baton.

'One six is six / two sixes are twelve / three sixes are eighteen / four sixes are twenty four / five sixes are thirty....' An emphasis signalled the half-way mark, the line brought to a peak before a satisfying conclusion could be reached. 'Eleven sixes are sixty-six, twelve sixes are seventy two.'

'Very good. That was well done. Ridgway, how many sixes in forty-two?'

'Five, sir.'

'Wrong. Anybody else?'

'Eight, sir?'

'Wrong. Let's do it again - this time we'll say it backwards. Ready? Twelve sixes are seventy two, eleven....'

Such rhythms defined Polly's week and ours, the same cadences spilling over into bells and breaks, chains and furlongs, censure and praise, prose and verse.

I must go down to the seas again, to the lonely sea and the sky,
And all I ask is a tall ship, and a star to steer her by,
And the wheel's kick and the wind's song and the white sails shaking,
And a grey mist on the sea's face and a grey dawn breaking.

The buses rumble, squalls fling salt spray against the wallcharts. From far away a seagull cries, and I'm on deck, whittling a piece of wood as the prow surges against the sky.

I must go down to the seas again, to the vagrant gypsy life,
To the gulls way, and the whales' way where the wind's like a whetted knife;
And all I ask is a merry yarn from a laughing fellow rover,
And a quiet sleep and a sweet dream when the long trick's over

I was back on land.

'Did you enjoy that poem? I've written the first verse on the board. Now I want you to copy it out in your best writing, then we're going to learn it off by heart.'

And we do.

Motes and chalk-dust spark in the afternoon windows, the summer classes torpid with heat and unshed jerseys, in winter chapped with cold and unshed snow. And into this rhythm comes yard games themselves defined by season: cricket, racing and shotties in summer; conkers in autumn, slides and snowball fights in winter.

The school, that cranky old man in black, took it all in his stride. He'd heard it all before. Snow, hail and rain, it was all one to him. We, just another lot, passing through.

Poem 'Sea Fever' by John Masefield 1878-1967.

CITY OF STOKE-ON-TRENT EDUCATION COMMITTEE

CHELL COUNTY BOYS' SCHOOL

REPORT
FOR YEAR July 1949

NAME: Ridgway William

Age: 9 years 3 months   Form/Class: J2A   Number in Frm/Class: 40   Position: 13

SUBJECT	Grade	Position	REMARKS	Initials
Religious Knowledge	G	—	V good	JH
English	V.g	4	very good work	JH
History	G	8	a very good result	JH
Geography	F.g	19	Fairly good	JH
Mathematics	V.fl.	26	very fair – improving	JH
General Science	V.Fl.	25	Interested	JH
Music	F.g	13/30	Fairly good	WJ
Art	V.g	39/40	very good work	JH
Craft				
Woodwork				
Metalwork				
Physical Training	G	18	Improving – more effort needed	JH
Games	g	—		
Reading	V. good.			JH
Writing	V good			
Spelling	F. Good.			

Height: 4' 7"   Weight: 5 st. 1 lbs.

Attendance: Ex   Punctuality: V good.

General Progress and Remarks:
Satisfactory work and progress throughout the year.

Date: 18 July 1949

H. Hanford — Form/Class Master
J. Quinton — Headmaster

A rare survival - my 1949 report signed by Form Teacher Mr Hanford.

12. A CLOSE CALL

I threaded my way through the ebbing Forties with a growing sense that things were getting better. My father now had a reasonable job, and his health had picked up. At the end of each month his mood would lighten as from his bag he took the reward for his labours in untaxed pound notes and florins - the tax burden endured nowadays part of an unenvisaged future. He'd allow us to lay them out on the table and count them, beaming like a fur-trapper who'd got a good price for his pelts.

By now I'd come to grips with the mini-world of which my school was part. To the side lay Pittshill Workingmen's Club flanked by its high stone wall, beyond it the yellow-brick sprawl of Hanley High School. In the opposite direction rows of smart houses ribboned High Lane, among them a shop dispensing liquorice roots and humbugs across a counter itself replete with bottled sweets. Also prominent in my Primary School world were the red double-deckers growling past the railings to Hanley, boys on delivery bikes and the odd Austin or Wolseley. This intimate tableau reached only as far as Chell Green Avenue, with its semis facing each other across an unadopted road.

I ran all the way home after morning school and ran all the way home again when the final bell sounded. Homework was never set, I carried neither books nor bag and I was usually unencumbered by either jacket or hat. At least one sock had ceded to gravity before I reached home, and my shirt had usually escaped the confines of my snake belt before I cleared the school gates.

None of this was of the slightest importance. A shirt, short trousers, socks and plimsolls comprised my wardrobe in those gloriously unselfconscious days, and my horizons were limited enough to avoid discontent, let alone pleas of deprivation.

Our evening meal was taken by the window overlooking the back 'garden', but we never ate until my father arrived home, his school bag fettered to his fingers though there was little in it but his lunch box and a copy of *Teachers' World*.

However, one afternoon I was greeted by a less comfortable homecoming. At the time, my mother was pregnant with my sister. Up until then her confinement had been without complications, but now I arrived to find her in pain with my father at her side. He wasn't usually due in until later. Clearly there was an emergency, and it was connected with childbirth, with her call of distress as I came in and an assertive knocking at the door which followed my arrival.

My father motioned for me to answer. Mrs Edmondson, our neighbour from the house opposite, made a brisk entrance.

'Is your mum in the front room?'

'Yes, she's having a baby. My dad's with her.'

Now in full mid-wife mode, she strode through, me following.

'Have the waters broke?'

'A few minutes ago. Thanks for coming. Can you look after her while I make a call?'

The brief exchange between my father and our neighbour was adult territory, a place I didn't stray into. But although I didn't understand the words, I understood the urgency behind them. Did things go wrong when women were expecting? Was this normal when babies came, or was there some unknowable problem I couldn't come to terms with? Had my dad called on Mrs Edmondson when he got back, who sent for him anyway, why was my mum calling out in pain, what was going on and why?

Dad took his coat from the peg and went out. 'I'm just slipping up to the phone box. Mrs Edmondson'll stay here till I get back.'

'What's wrong with mum?'

'She'll be alright. She's gone into labour. The baby's just a bit early, that's all.'

'What d'you mean?'

He stepped out without answering, leaving the door behind him open, almost breaking into a run down the path. He was always at his best in a crisis. Everyday life jaded him, and it was such moments of high tension that got the adrenaline flowing. He reached the phone box on the corner of Vicar's Road. I could see him dialling from the window. My mother was standing with her back to the mantelpiece. Mrs Edmondson was supporting her, offering what help she could. With every pulse of pain, my mother cried out. There was nothing I could do but watch in anguished silence.

'Don't worry, the ambulance won't be long,' said Mrs Edmondson.

'How long?' I asked.

'Not long.' My mother let out a yell. 'Hang on just a bit longer, May, Bill's just gone to phone the ambulance. Try not to worry. It'll soon be here.'

My father came back in. 'About ten minutes they said. How is she?'

'She's doing fine, aren't you May? Bill says they'll be here in ten minutes.'

My mother's labour pains had subsided, but for how long? Would they begin again, and when? Would the ambulance get here in time, would she have to have the baby there, in the living room, or would they take her to hospital? I went out the back and looked for something to do. I found a stick and swished at the grass in a vain attempt to blot out the panic which had gripped the afternoon and threatened to stifle it. Down went the stick, the grass flew, the thistles lost their heads, the docks lay crippled underfoot. Then I heard bells ringing. I dropped the stick and went back in.

'I can hear it.'

'Where is it?'

'Coming up High Lane.' I went over to the front window, looked through the nets. 'It's outside now!'

'Better let them in,' said Mrs Edmondson, as my mother, afflicted anew with pangs of pain, let out another cry.

Now there were people in uniform and the house was full of advice and blankets. I caught a last glimpse of my mother being helped down the path. Then the ambulance doors were slammed, Mrs Edmondson had gone and the house was still.

'Where's she gone, dad?'

'Up the City General. She'll be alright.'

My dreams that night were untroubled. But when I awoke early next morning I remembered, and went downstairs to find my father dressed to go out.

'What's happened to mum?' I ventured.

'I phoned up the hospital in the night. You've got a sister. Your mother's decided on Jacqueline!' I struggled to come to terms with this latest development. 'We're going to see her. There's a taxi on its way, so you'd better get your skates on.'

Two weeks later, my mother arrived back home with the new arrival. I never mentioned it at school, ran all the way home for lunch and tea, knew that life would run its course no matter what I did or said. We were now a family of five.

Though I didn't know it then, I was to be spared any similar surprises in future.

Cousin Lawrence with Aunt Flo (left) and Aunt Anne.

3. A NEW DECADE

The Forties were drawing to a close. Mr Attlee was still in charge of the country, and a jet airliner called the Comet had taken to the skies. They were showing *The Red Shoes* at Barber's Picture Palace, and I'd discovered magic painting books and flies - trapped on sticky tape fixed to the ceiling of Frank Danby's shop.

The Fifties were on their way. I'd be ten. If I was lucky I might glimpse one of the new American-styled cars: a Standard Vanguard, an Austin A 40, a Vauxhall with its silver-fluted bonnet. Still in black, of course, but a far cry from the pre-war bolt-winged Rileys, Rovers and Austins parked behind Tunstall Market on Saturdays. The wind of change hung in the air, and my nose twitched in anticipation.

Perhaps my parents were less caught up in this psychological time-leap. Many of their routines were still bound up not only in the Forties, but in the Thirties and beyond. Our council house might have had a bath, but there were still quarries in the kitchen which my mother mopped much as my Tunstall grandma had done since her marriage a generation ago. And my mother still used fire-warmed irons to smooth out the creases and a rack over which freshly ironed garments were folded before being hoisted to the ceiling. Our out-house, too, harboured the relics of a pre-war life, including a cobbler's last which dad still used for tipping our shoes when money was tight. Still, the new decade was firmly in sight. What would it have in store for me, I wonder?

Chapters

1. The Tunnel

2. In Service

3. A Step Change

4. Remote Vision

5. A Home Visit.

6. Time to Spare

7. Winners and Losers

8. Birds in the Attic

9. A Buckled Wheel

10. Ragabo's Chick

11. Back to St Mary's, Back to Chell

My brother Mike looks pleased with himself outside my grandparents' Lime Street home around 1949

1. THE TUNNEL

During my mother's confinement, my brother Michael had spent some days at our Tunstall grandma's. Now he was back home aiming to make up for lost time, and not many weeks elapsed before his introductory venture.

The tunnel which carried the mineral line from Chatterley Whitfield Colliery ran under the High Lane ridge. A steam vent had been built half way, its tower situated in the garden of a bungalow almost opposite our school gates. Anyone standing near the outlet would hear the low rumble of an engine entering the tunnel, and a thin cloud of steam would rise from the tower, marking the train's progress.

Much to the annoyance of the 'authorities', it wasn't only coal trains which made use of the tunnel. Local youths frequently did the trip, making it a venue for freebooters after fallen coal, freewheelers seeking adventure and freeloaders looking for a free ride. Over time a friction developed between those who'd 'done the tunnel' and those who hadn't; there was also rivalry between those who'd 'been right through' as opposed to the half-way mark. However, particular respect was reserved for the ones who'd shared the tunnel with an oncoming train, a procedure accomplished only by the brave and the deaf.

Shortly before his eighth birthday my brother was invited to add his name to this illustrious list, though it's doubtful whether he knew much about the challenge when he volunteered. He'd tagged on to an older gang, several of whose members had already been through, one reported to have made the trip hanging on the back of a wagon. Now it was Michael's turn to prove his status on the street by doing the 'doffer'.

He had a rudimentary idea that this wasn't something you were supposed to do, and that it could be hazardous if you tried to do it. He also had the feeling, even at that age, that the track below the footbridge where he and his cronies were now gathered was no mere railway line, but a pathway to glory. The time had come, the course set. He'd do it.

The route into the cutting was well known, and after a furtive glance up and down they rolled commando-style under the fence and onto the track. The mouth of the tunnel lay some hundred yards ahead, and they made their way towards it keeping their heads down and signalling for quiet when anyone was clumsy enough to dislodge a lump of shale. Now the cutting had become a canyon whose sheer walls plunged both track and travellers into a secluded netherworld of abandoned hawsers, decaying fence posts and rusting prams.

The light had faded to an oppressive gloom, the mouth of the tunnel yawned, the traffic noise abated. Now they were ready to chance their arm by moving their feet. At the entrance they craned forward and peered into the cavernous interior. Far ahead, a glimmer of light marked the other end. Just beyond it lay Little Chell Lane and Tunstall Park. It was time to go.

Michael's later account of his progress through the tunnel contained not only much of the above, but provided a detailed description of what happened after the third member of the group 'chickened out', leaving only him and a fellow fantasist to complete the journey.

'It's bigger than it looks but you'll soon get used to it.' Michael's friend flicked on the torch he'd brought. 'See? It's only five minutes to the far end.'

'Can we go back, now?'

'Don't worry, there's no train.'

'How d'you know it won't come?'

'I can't hear a train, can you? Anyway, there's holes in the wall. You can hide in one of them if a train comes.'

'What happens if someone gets us?'

'Who?'

'The police from Whitfield.'

'What're you on about? There're no bobbies in Whitfield. Anyway, the police won't come down here. They're not daft. It's pitch black for a start. Listen!' The friend called out and waited for the echo, which, when it came, added further to my brother's growing sense of unease. 'Come on, Mick. You're best treading between the lines, there's puddles by the wall.'

They'd almost gained the base of the air shaft when a distant clanking came from the direction of the park.

'A train's coming,' Michael said, signalling urgency with an unseen hand. 'Shall we go back now?'

'No, it isn't. It's just a lorry you can hear....Hey! You're right. It *is* a train. Come on, Mick, let's get out!'

'I can't see where I'm going. Give us the torch.'

'I'll keep the torch. Last one out's a cissy!'

The leader's observation reverberated down the tunnel. The clanking grew louder and Michael, deprived of the torchlight which accompanied his friend towards the exit, stumbled about in the dark. He missed his footing, stumbled, grubbed about in the oily wet. He was on his own. Daylight wasn't far away, and it had never been so welcome.

Now he was out and running as best he could, for he'd grazed his knees and cut his hands. There was a faint rumble as the train plunged into the tunnel. He gained the foot bridge. His ex-friend was nowhere to be seen. Now the cutting was shallow, and he found the runnel of scuffed ash which marked his exit route.

He was climbing under the fence when *Edward,* one of the pit tankers, emerged from the tunnel in a plume of steam. He thought of waving to the driver, then decided a wiser course might be to hoof it back home. He'd had enough excitement for one day.

When he got in, my father was waiting for him.

'I want a word with you. I've been told you were down the tunnel.'

'I wasn't. Who told you?'

'Never mind who told me. Have you been there or not?'

'I was only playing.'

'Who was with you?'

'Some big boys.'

'Why are your trousers all sludged up? What have you been up to? Don't you know it's dangerous?'

'It was full of water.'

'What if a train had come?'

'What's for tea?'

My father had an uncommonly long index finger, which he now employed to jab at my brother's chest. 'I'll tell you what's for tea. If I find you playing down there again, I won't be responsible for my actions, that's what's for tea. Do you understand what I'm saying'

'What's he mean, mum?'

'It's no use you asking your mother. Now go upstairs to your room and wait until I tell you to come down.'

He went. After that he didn't seem so keen on 'doffers'- or, at least, my father never got to hear about them.

2. IN SERVICE

Dr James Richmond lived in a large, detached house off Little Chell Lane. Smartly dressed, urbane and courteous, he was one of those Ronald Colmanesque figures who epitomised a certain sort of Fifties middle-class professional, popping up at whist drives, golf courses, staff-rooms and hotel lounges and living in the more affluent parts of the city. Well-spoken and kindly disposed, Dr Richmond belonged to this elite band, the deference which came his way as much to do with him as his rung on the social ladder.

In light of this, it was something of a surprise to find his first name reduced to a swashbuckling 'Jimmy'. His glamour was such that this familiarity gave him and his career a racy gloss. Plain Dr Richmond was shirt, tie and Rover saloon. *Jimmy* Richmond, on the other hand, was cravat and sports car.

He shared a surgery off Tunstall High Street with a Dr Howie. Our own Dr Halpin held his surgery in what was once a stable in the grounds of a red-brick Victorian house below Christ Church, and it might have been through him that my mother got to hear of the cleaning job at Jimmy Richmond's.

With my brother and me at school, and my sister at the local nursery for a few hours a week, my mother thought the pin money she'd earn at Dr Richmond's would be a useful addition to the housekeeping. She hadn't worked since her London marriage - at the time she'd been employed by Black Cat cigarettes, a then state-of-the-art factory known as the Arcadia Works in London's Mornington Crescent. My arrival in the second year of the war, my brother's four years later, had curtailed any likelihood of full time work in the foreseeable future. A few hours spent cleaning for someone wasn't ideal, but it was money, and along with the wage came a measure of independence.

Jimmy Richmond's wife, Joan, organised mum's day. Joan was not unlike the village matriarchs portrayed by Agatha Christie. Dressed in a tweed suit and a fashionable felt hat, the house was her province and according to my mother little went on there she didn't know about, or get to know about. The Richmond children were brought up to respect the etiquette of their class and time, codes of acceptable behaviour enforced by that combination of fair-mindedness and firmness which was then part of a school's ethos too.

My mother's duties lay in cleaning whichever of the large, high-ceiling rooms had been prescribed by Mrs Richmond on the day. It was on one of her weekly stints that she had first hand experience of the no-nonsense approach to household discipline employed by the doctor's wife.

Coming to the end of her work, she heard a raised voice coming from the back garden. It was Mrs Richmond's.

'You have been very naughty, both of you. I'm most surprised at you.'

What had the children done? Broken something? Lost something? Played out of bounds?

'You know what I said, don't you? Well? What did I say?'

A hushed, repentant reply was given.

'And what d'you say?'

'Sorry, mummy.'

'I'm most disappointed in you. Now go and stand in the drawing room and wait for me there.'

My mother watched the children from the kitchen window. After an interval, Mrs Richmond followed. A muffled admonition continued from the next room.

'Now you admit you've been naughty. Because you've owned up, I shall be lenient with you this time, but don't let it happen again.'

'No, mummy.'

There followed two faint slaps.

'I'm very proud of you for owning up. And you've taken your punishments very bravely. The matter is now closed. You may have a biscuit each from the tin and go out to play.'

The children reappeared in the back garden. The doctor's wife came into the kitchen. 'Are you off, then, Mrs Ridgway?'

'I've got to go and collect my daughter now, Mrs Richmond. I think you'll find everything's in order.'

'I'm sure it is. I'm afraid it's been one of those days. D'you ever have them?'

'All the time.'

My mother never knew what the fuss had been about, but the episode made a lasting impression on her, and she couldn't help but compare it to my father's less formal confrontation with my brother after Michael's visit to the tunnel a couple of weeks earlier. She may even have been a little in awe of Mrs Richmond, whose clear-cut parameters of conduct were enforced with kindness, thus sparing her children the neurosis of licence - along with its bed-fellow, neglect.

However, her stint at Jimmy Richmond's didn't last long. Class was my father's *bete noire*, and her job working for someone he considered a notch up the ladder rekindled feelings of his own insecurity. This assessment of his social position was more a result of genes and upbringing than the unwelcome truth that he, too, was now a professional man, a category shared by the Richmonds and Richmond wannabes in their semis.

These complex cerebral gymnastics were lost on me as a child, and though I'm now able to articulate them, one can never fully tease out the small-print underlying others' motives. It seems likely that echoes of a previous generation of girls 'in service' was still shaming in his eyes. She relinquished the work and the pin-money that went with it. In fact, but for a brief stint in the school kitchens at Chell, she took no further paid employment.

Some time later, the Richmonds moved. The house where they lived, and where my mother did her few hours a week, is today much as it was when they could see *Polly* or *Roger* drawing the coal trains across Little Chell Lane from their front garden.

Dr 'Jimmy' Richmond's home Sunnyside Avenue, Tunstall.

3. A STEP CHANGE

My days at Chell Primary were numbered. A new school at Chell Heath was almost complete. Chell, like St Mary's before it, had become familiar territory. I was the fastest sprinter in my class, an accident of height and length of stride rather than ambition. My reading was 'coming on', my number-bonds 'weak but improving'. Would this new school be more of the same, or different? Why was I moving half-way through my Primary days? The machinations of the adult world were not to be questioned. I was a pawn in the hands of Powerful Others and blissfully unaware of it.

'Your first day tomorrow,' my mother announced. 'I'll walk down with you if you like.'

I didn't like. 'Why do I have to go?'

'It's a new school. Your father thinks it'll be better.'

'Why?'

'I think he knows one of the teachers there.'

After breakfast next day I felt in my trousers for my cigarette cards - a comforting talisman I'd pocketed the night before - and set off.

Chell Heath Juniors represented a self-conscious desire to embrace the optimism of returned peace. The high-raftered formality of the Board Schools had been edited to a series of single-storey blocks, each with a planted area and an expanse of glass unknown to a pre-war generation. The school was cutting-edge and knew it; the walls were off-white and on-message, the straw-board ceilings almost within touching distance. It was draught-free and spacious both inside and out, and framed prints - there was even a Picasso - were part of the package.

Along with the Standard Vanguard and Dior's New Look, schools had taken a step-change. After cramped St Mary's and spartan Chell, my new school had taken on the character of a cheerful ice-cream seller, welcoming me with a well-topped cone. I had no need of cigarette cards or any other supportive gimmick. I joined Tommy Stringer in the line and entered on the bell, free at last from exhortations to march.

Miss Martin was our class teacher and my first brush with glamour. Had I known about Grace Kelly, I'd probably have envisaged Miss Martin in that role, her hair fashionably adrift above the wheel of an open-topped car as she nudged eighty through the Dolomites. She was as much a product of 1950 as the school: manicured, wishing to make something of itself, set for better things. Far from the reaches of Polly, I found myself in a different arena, with a woman's finger on the pulse and no minutiae of the school day overlooked. Miss Martin would listen when you told her you had no red paint left, and provide a replacement. With the men you'd still get the replacement, but it took longer to reach you and you got the impression they'd rather be indulging some private passion of their own - a gender trait I recognise in myself.

Miss Martin was friendly with Mr Pipe, the Headmaster, and in odd moments they could be seen engaged in conversations which may have had less to do with the state of contemporary education than the state of a shared golf course. Mr Pipe, too, was glamorous, more debonair than Polly, less chalky. A tall, athletic-looking man, I remember him retrieving a boundary ball in one of our cricket matches. Grey hair and horn-rims apart, he appeared younger than his years; a new man for a new age, the future the only place to be.

Art lessons were Miss Martin's stock-in-trade. Languourous afternoons drifted by in painting, the only sounds the tinkle of brushes in the water-filled jam jars, the whispered encouragement of the teacher, the faint beat of plimsolls in the bee-torpid air.

'To make orange, you mix red with yellow, like this.' A demonstration would follow, shades of varying strengths produced and discussed. 'What does this remind you of, William? Can you think of anything?'

'The sun, Miss.'

'Very good, William; the sun. Anything else? Yes, Christina?'

'Please, Miss, our ginger tom, Miss.'

'But ginger toms have other colours as well. Can anyone tell me what they are? Yes, Albert?'

'Please, Miss, black, Miss.'

'And what does a ginger tom do, do you think?'

'It prowls, Miss.'

'Our cat catches mice and leaves them by the door.'

From the skein of such exchanges emerged the yarn which would give form to our painting, Miss Martin's skill the trick of teasing out a theme she'd already decided while listening with half an ear to Mr Pipe.

'This afternoon, then, I'd like you all to show me how well you can paint an animal picture. It can be your pet, your rabbit or cat or dog - even a tortoise if you have one. Or it can show the wild beasts of the forest, hunting their prey in the dead of night. Or even fishes in the sea. And I want to see the painting with the best orange colour in it.'

Miss Martin's ambitions also extended to handicraft, thereby increasing her chances of chaos by a considerable degree. Balking neither at paste nor scissors, she'd pre-empt disaster by issuing instructions of such whittled-down simplicity, even the most inept of us could be assured a production worthy of a Bond Street gallery. A favourite was the creation of a vase from a jam jar, an introduction to papier mache part of the process. Again, Miss Martin would demonstrate each stage, laying out the tools of her trade across her desk as we gathered around.

'You've all brought your newspapers?'

'Yes, Miss Martin.'

'And your jars?'

'Yes, Miss Martin.'

'First we tear out a sheet from our newspaper and cut it into narrow ribbons, like this.' She'd cut a strip with blunt-ended school scissors, laying it conspicuously across the desk so no one would complain they hadn't seen it. 'Your strip can't be too wide. This strip is about right. Next, you paste it, and make sure you don't get too much paste on your brush or it'll be all over the place.' Again, a demonstration followed. 'And now, very carefully, you stick the strips round your jar beginning at the top and working your way to the bottom. What did I say, Jimmy?'

'I can't remember, Miss.'

'Beryl, you tell him.'

Beryl did.

'Can you remember that, Jimmy? Next time pay attention instead of talking to Alan Gibson. Now I want to show you what your jar should look like when it's finished.'

Miss Martin would fish in her desk and produce the highly decorated fruit of last year's labours before an admiring audience.

'What does this remind you of?'

'Please, Miss, a vase, Miss.'

There was more in the same vein, a souffle of knowledge lightly whisked, of pleasure without pressure, the unwritten codes understood by all and trespassed upon only rarely. I saw no reason why Miss Martin and Mr Pipe shouldn't have been burdened with nicknames. After all, our teachers at Chell not only had them but knew them by heart. Pipe in particular could have been made something of by the more inventive - Puffer, Smokey or even Specky Four Eyes promising candidates. It was not to be. Mr Pipe remained just that. And Miss Martin, who might have been Budgie, Tweet, or Pecker, never deviated from Miss Martin, just as Miss Featherstone and Miss Riley had been spared four years earlier.

4. REMOTE VISION

My mother's involvement with the Richmonds was no more than a grace note to the tune of our lives. Such inconsequential events ran through the grain of our history - a tin can being kicked along the pavement; newly-planted saplings along Sprink Bank Road; Santa in his coach; Sunday walks in Bradwell Wood - snapshots in the album of the mind which define a place and time.

I remember thinking in 1950 how modern the world suddenly seemed. The Forties had flicked by like the card squares in a rotating desk calendar. It was a new era, and felt like it. At school, those few pupils still in clogs, their noses streaming, already seemed marooned in an earlier era. I'd managed to steer clear of clogs, and by this time I had a piece of rag on standby. But my two shirts and jersey had seen better days, which to some extent aligned me with both camps, a position I've found it expedient to adopt at various times throughout my life.

My mother's darning mushroom was rarely packed away, and her sewing and knitting needles were frequently active on our behalf. She took it all in her stride, part of a weekly cycle spiced with snatches of song, observation and comment. Long before Lennon and McCartney penned *Here Comes the Sun*, after a spring shower she'd open the front door, sniff the air, and as the clouds began to brighten, exclaim: 'Oh, don't it smell lovely and sweet now this rain's stopped. Here it comes. Here comes the sun. God's in His Heaven and all's right with the world.'

Like my Tunstall grandmother, she had a litany of such stock phrases, and a mournful eye for the demise of the rich, the famous and the infamous. Among the notables of her pre-war days whose own days were numbered was Ivor Novello. I remember her listening to the Home Service when the announcement was made, and her comment: 'I see poor old Ivor's gone.' (1951) This was followed a couple of years later by: 'I see poor Al Jolson's dead' and in the same year: 'They found all them poor women in a cupboard' on hearing about the Christie murders. Her flare for the macabre had been honed some years earlier by the Hague killings ('He used to dissolve the bodies in acid, but her handbag wouldn't dissolve and that's how they got him.')

Normally level-headed, she'd developed an instinct for the chilling, able to distil a lengthy account into a single lurid statement which she would later relay to anyone within earshot. Perhaps she'd inherited this tendency from her own mother, who as a young girl living in London's East End at the time of the Jack the Ripper murders, had told her: 'No one went out after dark, the streets were deserted.'

However, telepathy was her defining characteristic - particularly involving her twin sister, who was then living in Hillingdon in the north London suburbs. On numerous occasions mum would 'get the impression all's not well with Ivy' and a telephone call from the box on the corner would confirm her suspicions.

'Hello, Ivy, this is May.'

'Hello, May, I've just been thinking about you.'

'I'm phoning to tell you to be careful. Have you done anything to your shoulder lately?'

'How did you know that? I tripped over this morning while I was making the bed. I got it all bandaged up.'

'Is it alright?'

'It's just a bad bruise. It should be gone in a day or two. It's pretty sore at the moment.'

'I thought something must have happened. That's why I rang up.'

'You should get a job on the stage, you'd make a fortune.'

Such exchanges happened frequently enough for me to consider them normal, and I accepted my mother's 'gift' as readily as the mysteries of wireless and the telephone she'd called from. At times, instead of a call of corroboration, her unease could take the form of a faulty premonition:

'Hello, is that you, Ivy?'

'You sound worried. Is everything alright up there?'

'It's not about me, it's about your Pauline. You want to watch out for your girl. I've a feeling something's going to happen to her. Just take care, will you?'

'How did you know that?'

'How did I know what?'

'She got hit by a car yesterday.'

'No! She did what?'

'She got knocked down by a car.'

'Is she alright?'

'Well, she's got her arm in plaster 'cos she broke it. Apart from that she's fine.'

'I knew something was brewing. You can't be too careful. You'll have to tell her to watch out in future.'

My mother took her unusual sideline for granted and felt no reluctance in recounting the unexplained in the same breath as 'I see poor old Ivor's gone.' She told me how she knew her brother Harry had been killed before Lord Haw-Haw's announcement on war-time radio that *HMS Cornwall* had been sunk by the Japanese in the Indian Ocean.

'At that time you didn't know what to believe. Not with Lord Haw Haw, you didn't. One day he told you a pack of lies and the next he told you the truth. You were never sure one way or the other. But I knew already, so he was wasting his breath.'

'How did you know?'

'I'll tell you what happened. Harry came to me in a dream. He told me, "I'm going now, May. I shan't see you again. Don't worry about me, just take care of yourself".'

She recounted the dream, remembered years later, with the quiet assurance that leaves no room for doubt. As she grew older, her telepathic experiences seemed to happen less frequently, but every so often she could still surprise us.

I learnt at an early age, sitting with my bayko or reading a comic, that things aren't always straightforward. There's a lot more to it than that.

Mum, around 1936.

5. A HOME VISIT

The day my father came across an advertisement for entrants into teaching via the Emergency Training Scheme turned out to be his lucky break. He applied to Alsager Training College, and was interviewed by the Principal, Mr Woodiwiss. A week later he was offered a place on the one-year course. He started in 1946, a few months after our arrival in Chell Heath. Within the year he'd taken his first post at Summerbank County Primary School in Tunstall, catching the bus to school from the stop at the junction of Sprink Bank Road and High Lane.

It didn't take him long to adjust to his new job. Accepted at a relatively late age, (he was then 36) he was grateful enough for this reversal in his fortunes to make a pledge to whatever guardian angel had provided him with his first secure employment since the war.

My dad was now a teacher, and that carried some baggage. It had status, for a start. And we were expected to be on our best behaviour and 'not show him up'. Apart from the odd peccadillo, we didn't. But shortly after my move to Chell Heath Juniors, my brother had scarlet fever - with potentially damaging repercussions for my father.

Michael had been complaining of a sore throat since Monday morning, but my mother, used to his ruses, had made him go to school anyway. He continued to complain when he came home that afternoon, and now his sore throat was accompanied by a headache. By evening, he was in obvious discomfort and ready for bed. This was an alarming departure for someone who nightly had to be cajoled, sometimes threatened, to make his way upstairs.

My mother helped him undress; it was then she noticed the rash on his chest.

'Here, come and look at this.'

Michael was now subjected to a comprehensive examination by both parents and me. His chest, stomach and lower neck had acquired the sort of red tinge associated with sunburn.

'It's all over him. Shall we get the doctor?'

'How long have you had the rash?' my father asked.

Even in his sleepy state, Michael was beginning to enjoy the attention.

'Two days,' he managed, cultivating a weak croak in line with the seriousness of his condition. 'She made me go to school. I told her I was bad.'

'I'll make you a hot water bottle and tuck you in,' mum offered.
'Don't want a hot water bottle. I'm hot.'
'D'you want a drink of water?'
'Yes, I'll have a drink and go to bed.'

By now he was getting into his stride, milking the pathos for all it was worth. When he'd gone, my father said he thought it was scarlet fever, and if Michael was no better by the morning they'd send for the doctor. Next day, the rash had faded a little, but the patient was still groggy and complaining. My mother rang Dr Halpin.

Michael was in bed, leafing lethargically through a picture-book when the doctor arrived.

'So this is the patient, Mrs Ridgway?'

'He's been in bed all morning, doctor. He seems a bit better than yesterday, but he still feels weak.'

'Alright, young man, stick your tongue out.' Michael made a half-hearted attempt. 'No, that won't do, stick it right out.'

'Do as the doctor says, Michael.'

'That's better. My, you've got a tongue like a ripe tomato. Right, you can put it away and go back to reading your book. What's it called?'

'It's a magic painting book.'

'Very good. I see your mother's taking good care of you.'

Mum followed the doctor downstairs.

'It's scarlet fever. He's over the worst, should be gone in a day or so. Now, Mrs Ridgway, you must keep him at home for the week. It's best if he stays in his bed. I'll be back on Friday to see he's alright.' He opened the door. 'I'll have to fumigate the room. Good morning.'

Friday arrived, and Michael was pronounced ready for school the following week. Before he left, Dr Halpin lit a disinfectant wick, then sealed the bedroom door and window with tape. By now my brother was getting bored. Despite my mother's best efforts he'd decided he wanted to be out and about again. She went to hang out the washing and when she returned she glanced through the window and caught sight of him playing in the street.

At that moment a car pulled up. An official-looking man stepped out and made his way up the path.

'Mrs Ridgway?'

'Yes?'

'I'm the Schools' Attendance Officer for the area. I believe your son

Michael hasn't been to school this week. I'm just calling to see what's happened.'

My brother was kicking a ball along the pavement. My mother snatched furtive glances over the man's shoulder while wondering how to extricate herself from what was becoming a tense situation.

'He hasn't been well. He's had scarlet fever.'

'That's very infectious.'

'Yes, I know. He's spent all his time in bed.... he should be in school on Monday.'

'Thank you, Mrs Ridgway. We look forward to seeing him, then.'

He turned to go. At the same time Michael grew bored with football and decided it was time he went indoors for a drink. He passed the School Board Officer half way up the garden path.

'Hello? Are you Michael Ridgway?'

'Yes, I've been bad.'

'He only got better today,' mum blurted out in desperation. 'I told him to stay around the house. Short of nailing him to the floor, I can't see what else I could do to keep him occupied.'

The man now produced a fountain pen and a marbled book from his bag. 'He should really be in school now he's better, Mrs Ridgway, not on the streets. Is your husband at home?'

'No, I'm afraid he's out at work.'

'And where's that?'

'He's at Summerbank School.'

'He's a teacher?'

'I'm afraid so.'

There was little point in concealing the fact. She smiled sheepishly. The man's pen wilted on the page, but nothing was written and it was capped and clipped back in the caller's jacket. In the tone of one long unsurprised by what the day might bring, he said: 'Please make sure your son returns to school, Mrs Ridgway. It is important, you know.'

'Don't worry, I'll see that he gets there.'

And so the episode passed, one of many which spiced my brother's early life and rippled outwards to catch my dyspeptic father and long-suffering mother in its undertow. As for Michael - the incident was already history.

6. TIME TO SPARE

There was much to do in the idle hours. A jig-saw puzzle was usually available on a tray on the sideboard, with the straight edges set out ready to begin. When that was complete, the games came out - Tiddly-winks, Chinese Chequers, Hoop-la, Draughts, Ludo or Snakes and Ladders. Each was attacked with equal vigour when bad weather set in, and rivalries between my brother and me set in at about the same time. These games would first came to light in a pillow-case at Christmas, and lasted for years. Eventually the draughts got lost, the chequers fell down the sofa, the Tiddly-wink counters went astray and the Snakes and Ladders board became disfigured through use.

When I preferred my own company, I'd settle down with a book. By the early Fifties I'd learnt to read well enough to make sense of most of the material which came my way, which is not the same as saying a lot of books came my way, because they didn't. We had few books in the house, and where the ones which were available came from was an enigma ranking alongside the mysterious appearance of the piano, the marble clock and the Marie Celeste.

I spent many evenings engrossed in one such arrival - *The Wonder Book of Why and What,* a compendium of knowledge-made-easy with illustrations and black-and-white photographs that held my attention for hours. Its size marked it out for the kind of prestige lacking in the paper-backed folk tales with titles like *The Hobyahs* I'd come across at Chell Heath Juniors.

Also making its way into our sideboard was a volume of Arthur Mee's encyclopaedias, dating from before the war. When the mood took me, I'd trawl through that, passing from subject to subject as the mood took me. It wasn't the oldest book on the shelves however. Pride of place here was an edition of *Boys Own Papers*, again of unknown provenance. The tone of the stories, uplifting and moral, packed with adventure and adventurers, was Edwardian England in print. Richly illustrated with line-drawings and wonderful fold-out colour plates, this was the first book I reached for. The cover might have seen better days, the pages might be loose or torn and the content defined by Britain's place in a world which no longer existed. None of that mattered. It provided me with an escape route far beyond the backs and kept me enthralled for hours.

Then I discovered comics. Foremost in this new territory were the *Dandy* and *Beano*. Neither was delivered by the paperboy, since the family budget only ran to the *Evening Sentinel* and the *News of the World*. The comics I managed to come by were treats bought on shopping trips with my mother, together with a rare *Picture Post* or a women's magazine.

This newly-discovered world of anarchic humour was irresistible. I marvelled at the antics of Desperate Dan with his daily diet of cow pie, and looked forward to the latest ruse of prank-playing Korky the Cat. Dennis the Menace and his anthropomorphic dog, Gnasher, were off the street and off the wall. Loveably insubordinate and hyperactive, you'd be unlikely to find them meekly attending to Miss Martin's vase-making instructions - or to much else, for that matter.

Even these larger-than-life characters paled into insignificance compared to the Bash Street Kids, a bunch of grotesque misfits whose weekly fun in outwitting their long-suffering teacher sent me chuckling to bed. Once my comics had been read and re-read, I swapped them for others - a transaction which would no doubt be frowned upon by the comic's publishers, but was inevitable given my meagre resources.

Not only did the knock at the door signal a new read with no money changing hands; it also introduced me to *Topper, Beezer* and *Wham!* - rivals in humour which never managed to pull it off in quite the same way as *Dandy* and *Beano*. But by this time I wasn't only playing for laughs. I cast my line wider and hooked in adventure comics which weren't really comics at all, but narratives with pictures added. *Hotspur, Rover,* and *Wizard*, aimed at boys of my age and older, all competed for my attention. Like *Boys Own Papers*, their themes extolled the upstanding Brit who always came out on top.

But now *Rover* and *Wizard* were eclipsed by the new and innovative *Eagle*. I was at Chell Juniors when it came out, and any copy I acquired was prized above all the rest. This was partly due to the cost - an unhealthy 3d - but more to do with a format which was completely novel at the time. The *Eagle* came in a generous landscape design and the quality and scope of its illustrations left the rest standing. It rarely came to light when swappers called because I'd harvested what copies I had in my bedroom and nobody was going to get his/her hands on them. In fact, I'd begun to cut out the central pages showing the working parts of a locomotive, tank or jet fighter and glue them into a scrap book for future reference, and no one was going to get his/her hands on them, either.

The *Eagle* introduced me to Dan Dare, his side-kick Digby and their enormously-headed alien adversary, the Mekon. Dan was square-jawed, resolute, wholesome and British. His derring-do trips around the solar system provided a moral compass to his life and that of the reader and made the *Eagle* an overnight sensation.

Other comics, among them *Valiant* and *Lion*, reached the hall floor but never had quite the impact of the *Eagle*, though the high moral theme continued with war and football competing for glory - Roy of the Rovers a particular contender for the hero stakes.

So I was kept good, until in the end my comic phase petered out. The *Eagle* scrap book I'd painstakingly compiled joined the *Wonder Book of Why and What*, Mr Mee's encyclopaedia and *Boys Own Papers* in that strange parallel universe of odd socks, unclaimed umbrellas and lost keys.

Maybe it's still there, waiting to be re-discovered.

A new comic for a new age. I was at Chell Heath Junior when the Eagle came out in the early 1950s.

7. WINNERS AND LOSERS

I'd been at Chell Heath Juniors for little more than a year when there was a subtle change in Miss Martin's modus operandi. Although art and the kind of trivial pursuits we enjoyed had not entirely been abandoned, her lessons now were increasingly given over to literacy and numeracy. At the same time, her vocabulary began to bristle with hitherto ill-understood words like 'test', 'marks', 'position', and eventually, 'Eleven Plus'. I found myself caught up in a bid to encourage 'promising pupils', who were despatched for 'special coaching' to Mr Pipe's office, where the head himself took the reins.

This time the conversation between Miss Martin and he might well have centred around this examination, the most important event in the calendar and a mark of prestige for the school that 'got them through'. The small band of us kicking our heels under his table represented the school's best hope. Here we were crammed full of information: not unlike the cramming that went on at the dinner table, instead of food our salvers came burdened with problems, leaving Mr Pipe with the problem of getting us to sort them out. This he did by gauging the kind of questions we'd shortly be confronted with and going over them ad nauseam until the method was secure.

There was talk of an Intelligence Test involving the sort of conundrums that had been doing the rounds since the Thirties: Dog is to kennel as pig is to.... Mary is to Tom as girl is to.... as well as a more direct assault on culture, vocabulary and memory in such questions as: Give another name for a heavenly body.... What name is given to a play set to music?

Those who opted for Marilyn Monroe and the Billy Cotton Band Show were unlikely to attract a high score. Yet off-beat answers were my stock-in-trade. I wasn't one of those intuitive exam-passers who knew instinctively what the examiner wanted and my interpretation of a question usually made little sense to anyone but myself. Still, I wasn't ejected from the group, so either Mr Pipe had detected a glimmer of promise or he was desperate for passes, no matter how unpromising the raw material.

Nor was Miss Martin to be outdone. English and Maths had taken on a new intensity. The words 'Eleven Plus' became both rubric and Rubicon, emblazoned on walls, Miss Martin's twin set and Mr Pipe's pipe. They were neon-lit and gave me the queasy feeling that failure meant relegation to the Second Division, success that you wouldn't have to go down the pit. I'm not sure such hazy perceptions made me work harder. Maths, never my strongpoint, resisted Miss Martin as it had Polly, and though I now knew my tables up to 12x, using them to get an answer was fraught with difficulty. *Betty receives 44 birthday cards and her brother Fred only 37. If it cost 1½d to buy a stamp for each card, how much change would there be from £1?*

Such arcane abstractions needed more than a margin of jottings. They needed someone who could empathise with the Maths, for a start, rather than Fred's diminished status. But Maths and the sort of logic that went with it had to be mastered, for the Eleven Plus was not just any exam; it was *the* exam, a triple-headed hydra that wasn't going anywhere until you'd taken the Intelligence Test. The other two, English and Maths, were only open to those who'd passed the first, those considered academically lacking unlikely to be called upon to sit any.

Never an ambitious family, I can't recall my parents urging me on. I went to school, did the work and came home - a pattern undisturbed by the passing years and the jobs I've done since. The poetry now delivered from Miss Martin's *Golden Treasury of Verse* had to be 'looked at'. Before, she'd read aloud to amuse, interest or induce sleep. Now those early delights were examined in detail, the text analysed and commented on:

> *Give to me the life I love,*
> *Let the lave go by me,*
> *Give the jolly heaven above,*
> *And the byway nigh me*
>
> *Wealth I ask not, hope nor love,*
> *Nor a friend to know me;*
> *All I seek, the heaven above,*
> *And the road below me*

'What is this poem about, do you think?' 'Is it sad or happy or both, and why?' 'What is more precious to the writer than a friend?' 'What does this tell us about the poet?' 'What does *jolly* mean? How can heaven be jolly?' 'What does *lave* mean, do you think? And what about *byway nigh me*?'

Had Stevenson known his stuff was going to be poured over be the likes of Miss Martin and me, he'd have set sail for the South Seas sooner than he did. I suppose there were excursions into rhythm and rhyme too, and as the weeks passed all aspects of the Eleven Plus seemed to merge into one. The Great Day approached, the more able more jittery than their counterparts on the other side of the academic playing field, but all a hostage to that accident of genes and fortune which would send a few to Brownhills High School for Girls and Hanley High School for Boys and the rest to the local Secondary Modern.

As for myself, I was less caught up in this mood of wary excitement which had gripped some of my companions. Had I been more applied, I could have cultivated the hunger necessary to achieve the best result. Had I been more aware of the future possibilities which success could bring, I might have run the extra mile. I didn't slack, but the neurotic clamour which nowadays attends schools in general and exams in particular was not part of my make-up. I plodded on by day, played by night, took the Intelligence Test - and failed. I was out on my ear, down at the first hurdle. Christina Leek, Joan Mayer, John Baddeley, Derek Rogers had all made it through, with Grammar School places in the bag. I didn't and hadn't.

At the time I took it in my stride. I was too young to be upset. I flew my kite over the backs without a backward glance. Exams were no part of my den-building, skylark-watching, cricket-playing life. I failed because I failed and life went on, any regret I might have had soon ousted by whatever a new day might bring.

It took some time before the truth dawned. I'd been given an opportunity granted to no previous generation. Neither money, background, nor class was as relevant as ticks on a sheet. For a bright boy whose father, but for a stroke of luck, might have spent his days red-leading hoppers, it could have been the first step to Better Things. I'd been offered a passport and blown it.

It would be tempting to say I learnt from my mistake, or learnt to be less cavalier with other chances that came my way. I did, but only for a time. Six years later, the Hidden Planner was back to his old tricks. I'd grown a lot but matured little. Perhaps the motley band of 'creatives' to which I suppose I belong doesn't easily fit the prevailing orthodoxy. Or maybe we're just a short-sighted bunch.

'You must take the rough with the smooth,' I hear my mother say.

And she was right. Though the way I saw it then, it wasn't as rough as all that.

Poem extract from R L Stevenson's *Songs of Travel - The Vagabond*

8. BIRDS IN THE ATTIC

Now reunited, my brother and his cronies decided on an explorative trip to Burslem Park. This was foreign territory, since the nearer park at Tunstall was the usual destination for people living around Chell. Despite his earlier escapade and the subsequent 'dressing down' he'd received from my father, Michael was once more confident his associates, who knew where they were going and what they were doing, would provide him with a few hours' entertainment. As it turned out, his faith in them was misplaced. Part of the fun was taking a short cut into the park via the railings. His friends had no trouble clearing the spikes, but they were canny and Michael was short. Squeezing through the gap seemed the better option, and that's where he came unstuck - or, to put it another way, stuck. By the time he'd got his head through the bars and realised they were too close for the rest of him, it was too late. He tried to pull out, but his ears got trapped and now his mates were out of sight.

Eventually one of them turned back, saw the problem and said he was going to look for something to prize back the railing so Michael could extricate himself. This wasn't easy, since by this time my brother's predicament was beginning to attract attention from a variety of passers by, including the park keeper.

After reprimanding him for not making his entrance via the gate like most normal people, the park keeper went off to search his tool shed - watched from the bushes by the rest of the gang. It was decided at this point that it might be a good idea to alert my father, and with this in mind one of them set off back to tell him the good news.

This was greeted with the usual resignation by my father, who pulled on his jacket and, since it was Sunday with few buses running, set out to walk to the park. No doubt muttering to himself as he made the two mile journey past Hayward's Hospital, and down Hamil Road, he now saw in the distance, not the group of bystanders he'd expected, but a solitary figure coming his way. It was Michael, recently released by the park keeper and, as before, minus his friends.

Dad waited. My brother approached. A reprise of the run-in after the tunnel incident, he neither anticipated a cordial greeting nor got it. My father's jabbing finger was no doubt employed to full effect at various stages on the way home to a late dinner. In the afternoon, after a further energetic reinforcement of the rules, Michael was allowed out to play while dad took his Sunday nap.

The next few days were fairly harmonious. My father continued at Summerbank, my mother had her hands full with my three-year old sister, my brother came back from school without mishap and I continued for the time being at Chell Heath Juniors. But during the following week-end this rare spell of calm was shattered.

It was Saturday, and we were on our way to Tunstall. All except my brother, who'd kicked up a fuss and after a lot of argy-bargy had been allowed to stay in and read his comics as long as he minded his own business, didn't use the stove, didn't have a bath, didn't mess anything up, didn't let anyone in or down. Before we went, my father spent some time specifying the conditions of their pact and outlining the reprimands likely to follow in the event of its being broken. My brother's show of indignation did nothing to allay the probing finger, or the doubt writ large on my father's face as we left the house.

According to later accounts, shortly after we set out for the bus stop the twittering began. At first it was an odd cheep, but this soon escalated to an insistent chirping which came from somewhere above. Michael put down his comic and climbed the stairs.

The noise could be heard even more clearly from the landing. His curiosity now fully aroused, he made up his mind to investigate further. After all, this mystery was happening not in a tunnel, or a park, but in his own house. The gang were wherever they were, there was no one else about and no rules had been breached since my father had said nothing about looking for birds in the attic - which was where the now strident chirruping was coming from.

The steps were brought in from the shed, manhandled up the stairs and under the hatch. He took the torch from a kitchen drawer and made his way back. The tools of the trade now in place, he pulled back the bolts which held the trap in place and pushed it gingerly upwards. Standing on the top step, he was able to direct a beam into the cavity, where it picked out only rafters. The warbling had now stopped, but he'd heard it before, might hear it again, and there was no one about to tell him he couldn't lever himself on to the nearest joist and have a poke around.

It was the first time Michael had been in our attic or any other, and he approached his task with unusual caution. The birds were now playing dead, so he had no clue as to where they might be nesting. In fact, he didn't have a clue about anything to do with attics, for his next manoeuvre took him between joists on to the plasterboard ceiling, through the ceiling and into my parents' bedroom.

Fortunately, he and a fair amount of debris landed on the double bed. None the worse for wear, he had the presence of mind not only to extricate himself from the shower of plaster which now covered the eiderdown, but to try to formulate a plan of action which would satisfy my father when he got home - and that wouldn't be long.

Michael was still turning things over in his mind when we got back. My mother noticed he was unusually quiet.

'Have you finished your comics?'

A plaintive 'Yes'.

Suspiciously: 'What's all that dust on your jersey? What have you been up to?'

That brought a sharp glance from my father.

'I went up to look for birds,' Michael ventured.

'And?'

'And I fell through the roof.'

Dad's finger froze, and he adopted his fall-back position, a rolling of the eyes intended to convey abandoned hope, disbelief and resignation. He disappeared upstairs, while we waited for the inevitable curses which would follow his discovery. We weren't disappointed.

Now the finger of retribution came out in style. As he was delivering his severest warning to date, I couldn't help but notice a dusting of powder where his sleeve had contacted the evidence. That night, as Michael slept an untroubled sleep, my father lay awake worrying what he was going to do about the hole above his head. Then he had an idea. It would involve a deception, but only a minor one; a white lie, really. The following day he'd ring the council and tell them that *he*, not my brother, had been investigating birds in the attic (the 'birds' being nothing more than water pipes gurgling in an empty house). He'd tell them he'd put his foot through the ceiling by accident. That way my brother would be in the clear, my father wouldn't seem negligent, the ceiling would be repaired free of charge and life would go on as normal - whatever normal was.

And so it did. But just in case, my father kept his finger on red alert....

9. A BUCKLED WHEEL

We all carry our genes around in a suitcase from the time we're conceived; the trick is getting the right package. I was the first-born Steady Eddie who looked before he leapt, whereas my brother leapt first and often. He had caffeine buzz without the coffee, whereas the Bash Street kids provided my vicarious adventures from the comfort of an armchair. My survival has depended on one system or another, Michael's on his wits. He's the adventurer, I play it safe. If the chips were down, he'd be the one to survive. Our personalities were as fixed as the Pole Star from first memory and have little, if anything, to do with the way we were brought up.

My brother never took to cycling, but I did, and from the age of eleven my bike and I were inseparable. The rudimentary machine I first owned wasn't just a set of wheels; it was wheels set to go places and I took full advantage of them.

At around this time I'd mated up with Derek Rogers, a school friend who lived close by and who was equally enthusiastic about cycling tours into the great unknown. One of our first runs was to Knypersley Lake, a reservoir a few miles from our estate which had been built to supply water to the Caldon Canal - and hence to the Trent and Mersey. The outing itself proved a great success, but my luck almost ran out on the return journey - it could have been the last trip I made.

We weren't yet into our stride, having neither food nor drink and no saddle bags to carry them in. Neither of us owned a pump, and my brakes wouldn't pass any tests. Nevertheless, we were off down Sprink Bank Road, under the colliery line bridge at Fegg Hayes, on to the main road which would take us past Brindley Ford and its heaps of slag to the right turn we'd been told to take.

Leaving the winding towers of Black Bull Colliery behind, we hit Childerplay Road, then Greenway Bank, where a stucco mansion came into view partly hidden by trees. Mansions were in short supply on our estate, and it was much later that I learnt the house belonged to a Mr Heath, the great grandson of mining millionaire Robert Heath, who'd left his mark in the form of the slag tip and pit we'd passed earlier. From the house to the lake was downhill all the way.

We spent some time in this new land less than half an hour from Chell Heath. Here magical discoveries were to be made: the Warder's Tower and the bridge below it, the water tumbling over the weir, the mill with its pond - delights indeed for an 11-year-old boy who knew about Tunstall and Chell Heath and not much else. There was much to do on that first visit, and we lost no time in doing it. We explored the woods, heard the trout plop, watched the water plunge over the overflow and the birds wheel across the water. Who built that boathouse, and when? Who drove that passage into the hillside? Why was that stone-lined spring in the woods called Gorton's Well when it wasn't a well - and who was this Gorton, anyway?

We got no answers and forgot the questions because by now tea would be on the way at home and it was an uphill climb to get at it. We pushed our bikes up Greenway Bank, which made us feel hungrier still but taught us the first of the lessons every touring cyclist had to learn: buy a saddle bag and pack it with food and drink. (Subsequent mishaps also taught us the value of a couple of spanners, a map, a cape and a puncture repair outfit.)

We free-wheeled down the slope to Bemersley Road and it was there Derek made his suggestion: someone had told him you could take a short cut down Peck Mill Lane. He said it was downhill all the way and that it came out only a stone's throw from Chell Heath and food. It would knock ten minutes off the journey and avoid the main road. He'd walked part the way once, thought he knew how to get to it. My belly agreed, and after a short ride up Bemersley Road we cut off right and began our descent.

The lane was unexpectedly steep and winding, and my cycle gathered speed at an alarming rate. I had both brakes full-on, but the bike was losing its battle with gravity and the hedges to either side were beginning to blur. I negotiated the first of the bends, managed the next, but now the gradient was even steeper. I managed to shuffle on to the crossbar and drag my shoes along the tarmac in a vain effort to slow down. But the lane continued to plunge, and I plunged with it.

It was then I saw the bend looming - not one of the moderate curves I'd already taken but a right hander even Miss Martin wouldn't have cared to tackle in the Dolomites or anywhere else. To make matters worse, there was a bridge to negotiate and beyond it a tree the size of a sequoia. My feet scraping the road, my hands desperately clutching at brakes as well as straws, I cleared the bridge, hit the tree, blacked out and came to in a nettle clump.

Derek, who'd gone on ahead but turned back on hearing the commotion, stared at my bike. The forks had shared the impact with the front wheel and were bent back into the frame. The wheel had redesigned itself and parted from the machine. Not short of sympathetic one-liners, he said: 'Look at your bike.'

His observation fell on deaf ears. I was still sitting in the nettles, oblivious to their sting and numb to any other kind of pain.

I think he eventually noticed. 'Are you alright?'

'I don't know.'

'Should we phone the doctor?'

'I don't know.'

'There's a bloke looking.'

By this time I'd risen shakily to my feet. What remained of my bike lay in the verge. The man was from a bungalow which stood opposite the bridge. Now he unlatched his gate and came over to inspect the damage.

'Can you move your arms? Your legs? Pain anywhere?' I went through the motions. 'I'll ring for the ambulance. Better safe than sorry. Come in and sit down.'

He had a phone, and offered me and Derek a cup of tea while we waited. By the time the ambulance arrived I'd more or less recovered, and apart from a few abrasions there was no harm done. The bike was a different matter, and I have memories of hauling the wreckage back home later in the vain hope I could fix it.

I couldn't, of course. Its last journey was to the rag and bone man, who would no doubt sell on the unbuckled rear wheel which had already come from somewhere else. He should have been commended for this early example of recycling - in both senses of the word.

My brush with disaster had taught me another useful lesson: if you can't pull up, don't start out. It didn't put me off cycling, however, and I was soon on the move again.

Not down Peck Mill Lane. Not this time. Too many bends, too many nettles.

10. RAGABO'S CHICK

The title's misleading, and for all I know our rag and bone man was happily married with a brood of doting children. He appeared on the local streets most weeks, his horse as familiar with the route as a local copper. Whenever I saw him he seemed shrouded in debris, his creaking cart piled high with mangle cogs, steel frames, pans, kettles, old prams, chipped tin plates and car wheels. Shortly after my Peck Mill Lane episode, he added what was left of my bike to his heap, throwing it unceremoniously over the side of his cart before his next call.

I'm sure the rag and bone man was happy in his world of junk, though he took pains not to show it. His scuffed hands held the reins with understated assurance. His coat and cap, having lost any style, seemed to have absorbed the greys and browns of horse and cargo, together with the odd rust stain.

We knew he was coming when we heard his call, 'Ragabo'. This strange abbreviation carried effortlessly across the tin-tack houses and washing lines into our living room whether the windows were open or not, and gave us enough time to search the out-house for something he wanted and we didn't. My mother's boiler came to grief on his cart some years after my father and Ike had used it to recharge their glasses; a galvanised tub followed it, together with a range of unusable tools. If there really was money in scrap, Ragabo must have made a mint from our house alone.

We only collected a few pennies, and I'm sure our reward for handing him Tutankhamun's funerary mask would have been equally modest. But money wasn't the only thing. He cleared our junk, thereby performing a valuable service in cleaning the place up. And to show how enterprising he could be, at some stage in the early Fifties he came up with the idea of chicks instead of cash.

The idea was simple. He knew chicks were a novelty and the children who usually carted the lighter stuff to his cart wouldn't be able to resist them. This way they'd be able to avoid the taint of money and own a chick instead. How he came by these chicks I don't know. Maybe his brother had a farm. Now squeaks from the cage at his side were in competition with his cry of 'Ragabo', and as he got through his round the cage emptied and the cheeps died away.

He was not the first rag and bone man to move into macro economics. A year or so earlier, his predecessor had presented a goldfish in a jar to anyone willing to struggle with saleable tat. We christened ours Olly and found it one morning behind the couch, a carelessly despatched victim of our tom, a survivor of many battles and owner of a face like a rubble sack. Perhaps that should have taught me to take precautions.

I didn't. Our cat had gone to that everlasting hunting ground for which his life on the street had prepared him, and the box containing the chick was handed down to me in exchange for a pair of rusting garden shears. I listened for its cheep, then took it indoors.

Carefully, I placed the box on the table and opened it. The chick stared up, a yellow ball precariously balanced on a pair of over-sized legs. It cheeped a couple more times to make sure I knew it had arrived, but made no attempt to get out. My mother wasn't impressed.

'What made you bring it in here? What're you going to do with it?'

'I got it from the rag and bone man.'

'I know that. What's it going to eat?'

'I don't know.'

'Who's going to clear up its mess?'

'It's only little.'

The chick soon became part of the family. Like the cock before it, it took an instant liking to my mother and accompanied her in her household chores. It kept watch from under the table when she mopped the floor, from the hearth as she dusted the furniture and from the quarries when she washed the dishes. When she moved, it moved. When she went to the toilet it waited at the bottom of the stairs. Its favoured speed was a run. There's no doubt that as far as the chick was concerned my mother was mother hen.

We managed to get some bird seed, which seemed to supply its dietary requirements when supplemented with a few crumbs of bread. I provided a saucer of water and some toilet paper to clean up the mess my mother had mentioned on its arrival. It began to thrive, it fluffed out, its legs shrank and its body grew. The only thing that didn't change was its continuing loyalty to my mother.

Then it stopped running. It languished on the hearth rug and didn't cheep. If it was possible for chicks to look crestfallen, that's how it looked to me. In fact, it was on its way out. Was it something we'd done? Diet, no mates its own age, struck down by a mystery illness to which Ragabo's chicks were susceptible? No one knew.

Then my father had a hunch which, like many of his ideas, centred around the curative properties of alcohol. From a high kitchen cupboard no one was likely to look into, he produced a bottle of Bell's. Whether this had been left over from a previous Christmas or had arrived since, I wasn't to know, but in the Fifties whisky wasn't cheap. Nevertheless, in a gesture of magnanimity towards the ailing bird, dad added a measure to its saucer of water, picked up the chick and dipped its beak into the mixture. There wasn't much else to be done.

The following morning my mother's household companion was up and running as before. Whether its new lease of life was down to good fortune or scotch was not clear, but for most of that day it was on top form and never slacked.

Unfortunately, the good times didn't last. By evening a relapse had set in, and just before bed time it gave its last, weak cheep. The following morning it was buried with honours under the line prop, and I dare say it was already raring to go to that great poultry farm in the sky. As for Ragabo - he still plied his rounds, but without his cage of chicks. Maybe someone had tipped off the RSPCA.

Whatever the reason, any future pots and pans that came his way would make the donor a copper or two as before - to my mind a far more acceptable option.

11. BACK TO ST MARY'S, BACK TO CHELL

Failing the Eleven Plus meant I had to go to a Secondary Modern school. I wasn't entirely sure what that would entail, except that I knew I was on the last lap, educationally speaking, and that when I left I'd be fifteen and ready for work. I had no idea what I wanted to do; fifteen seemed such a remote age it never worried me that four year down the line I'd have a big decision to make.

I left Miss Martin and Mr Pipe to the next bunch of hopefuls and looked forward to the long summer holiday. But my father must have been busy on my behalf, for shortly before the end of the six-week break he announced I was to attend his Alma Mater, St Mary's Secondary School in Tunstall. This was a stone's throw from my old infant school, and would entail my taking the bus again from the bottom of the road, an odd choice considering the secondary school at Chell was on the doorstep.

It was no use arguing. My father insisted the school, with its strong Anglican ethos, would be in my best interest. So that is where, in the September of 1951, I had my first brush with secondary education. Wrenched from the domesticity of junior school, I found myself sharing the playground with 14-year-old proto-adults shortly to be destined for Platt's Brickyard or Grindley's packing shop. The teachers too, nearly all men, had a humourless, world-weary approach to the job. Here it was surnames only, the lessons delivered in no-nonsense tones and questions not invited.

The school felt shabby and oppressive. Hemmed in by the soot-blackened church on one side and a path to the brickyard on the other, the building looked out on the windowless walls of truncated streets. Even the playground, a windswept enclosure whose walls were a barrier between school and Bradwell Wood, was joyless and bleak. For the first time I felt I was in the wrong place.

I told my mother I'd rather go to Chell. My father put it down to 'teething trouble', but she took up my case and struck the right note: 'What's the use of him going all the way down there if he's not going to be happy? His work won't be no good if he don't like it. And anyway, it's too far, all that travelling....'

Perhaps it was 'my work' which clinched it. No matter how good the school's reputation, if it couldn't salvage something of my dwindling academic career, perhaps he'd be prepared to give Chell the benefit of the doubt.

At that time Chell Secondary Modern was housed in three large Nissen huts which shared a campus with Hanley High School. They were separated from the

Grammar School by a strip of rising land and connected by a flight of steps which served as an outpost for prefect patrols and a hot-spot, I later discovered, for winter snowball fights. The high school students enjoyed the status of grey flannels, a navy blazer and striped tie. Their identity and the school's was reinforced by the school crest, emblazoned on the pen-pocket of the blazer to advertise where you came from, what you were and what you hoped to be.

We of the secondary section had no such aspirations. Here the jersey reigned supreme, whatever its colour and condition. A jacket, too, was sometimes in evidence, and not infrequently had begun its life on someone else's back. The Grammar School lads had bulging satchels; we had a drawstring bag which held our PT kit.

At the time, Acting Head Teacher Mr Marshall was in charge of both schools, with an office on the lower floor of the Grammar School building.

'Please take a seat, Mrs Ridgway. And this is William?'

'That's right. D'you think you'll be able to take him?'

'Well, we're rather full, you know. What was the problem at his other school?'

'He didn't seem to take to it.' A pause. 'He wasn't settling in, and we'd heard good reports about this school from neighbours.'

'Well, they're not all angels here at Chell, you know.'

'It's just that I don't think he'll do any good at that other place.... it was my husband's old school.... I told him, it's a long way for the boy to travel....'

Mr Marshall didn't intend to allow my mother to fight my corner alone. Behind the unwavering smile he'd been giving me the once-over: disposition, height, weight - it was all there, being processed.

'And what about William? Do you think you'd be able to cope with another new start?'

'Yes, sir.'

'And you'd be happy to join us at Chell?'

'I think so, sir.'

'You think so?'

'I was at Chell Primary, sir. I liked it there.'

'The boys are much older here.'

'I know, sir.... they were in Tunstall, too.'

Mr Marshall's eyes had taken on a far-away look that could have represented indecision, chicanery, boredom, concession or even concussion. Concession won.

'Alright, we'll see how you get on. When can he start, Mrs Ridgway?'

'Would Monday be alright?'

'I think so. I'll just make a note.' He reached into his pocket for his fountain pen and wrote something on a notepad. 'You'll be with Mr Bowers in the second block, William. The school day starts at nine, so if you could be there by ten to, he'll sort you out.'

I had the notion that status came with covered knees, so by the time I'd joined the crew outside the classroom I was the proud owner of a pair of long trousers. The teacher, who'd not been in evidence since my arrival, now put in an appearance. He bent to unlock the door and the class tumbled in. I tumbled in with them.

Having got used to the airy lightness of Chell Heath Juniors, the curved interior of the Nissen hut came as something of a shock. Everything seemed neglected, even the teacher's table, which faced rows of pupils' desks. An attempt had been made to brighten the walls, but the paintwork was scuffed and bare. The windows on one side looked out on to the embankment separating our classroom from Hanley High School; on the other side cricket practice nets and playing fields ended in a drop to the road.

I found an empty seat and sat. Curious glances stole my way, but there were other diversions and interest soon waned. The teacher didn't bother to introduce himself. Although my name had appeared in the register, I began to wonder if he realised I was new to the class when an unused exercise book landed on my desk.

'Put your name on the cover. And write 1E ENGLISH under it.' Maybe this was his introduction after all. 'Oakes, give them out.'

A boy struggled with a column of text books trapped under his chin. He threw a copy on each desk, the book coming my way dog-eared through use.

'Page 73,' announced Mr Bowers. A hand shot up. 'Well?'

'Please, sir, there's no 73 in my book.'

'Share.'

My own book was mercifully complete. I looked down at a series of line drawings which, in sequence, suggested a story. Beneath them were matching descriptive sentences, a sentence for each picture - but the sentences out of order.

'What can you tell me about the first picture? What's happening there? Any ideas?' Silence. 'What does the first picture tell us? Mm? Any answers?'

A response was hesitatingly delivered from one of the desks, and the teacher fell on it as if he'd discovered a pitcher of water in the desert. 'That's correct. That's what we're looking at in picture one. KEEP YOUR EYES ON THE PAGE AND STOP MUTTERING AMONG YOURSELVES. That's better. Now, who can pick the sentence from the list at the bottom that describes the scene? Who's going to have a go?'

He panned the room, the figures to whom his plea was directed hoping they wouldn't be addressed by name, their eyes fettered to the page. I found I'd put my hand up. One by one heads turned towards me.

'Yes?'

'Please, sir....'

'Name?'

'Ridgway, sir. Please, sir, Susan's father has left the gate open and Susan has got out.'

Was the ensuing silence resentment or regard? Resentment I thought, and I wished the genie who'd decided I was going to volunteer had stayed corked.

'That is correct. Now, you've all had a start. What I want you to do is work out the order for the other sentences and write them down.'

An industrious calm settled on the class. One by one nibs were dipped into the small porcelain ink wells and the chosen sentence dutifully copied, right or wrong. No one looked my way, I laboured with the rest.

In fact, I laboured with similar tasks for much of that first day. When the final bell sounded, I thought things weren't so bad after all.

Hanley High School at Chell around 1951.
The three dark Nissen huts in the foreground housed the Secondary Modern pupils.

4. HOME AND AWAY

Although I'd been living in Chell Heath for five years, Tunstall was only a mile away, my father's family still lived there and we paid a visit most week-ends. Though Tunstall lingered in the shadow of Hanley, it had a parochial buzz of its own, and I felt comfortable there. In the early Fifties it still had something of a village feel; everyone knew everyone else and they'd meet at the same shops and venues, the Market Hall, the Square, Woolworth's, Naylor's, Burton's, the Ritz or Barber's Picture Palace.

More often than not, our excursions took us to my grandma's house, where we'd see my father's sisters Dorothy, Anne and Flo, and to St Mary's Church, where my brother and I were cajoled into attending the Sunday service. But there were also trips to Bradwell Wood, or to the cinema (when something was showing which caught my father's eye) and to the park, when the band was playing.

Tunstall 1950s.

Chapters

1. Musical Blacksmiths
2. Temples of Delight
3. Stained Glass and Brassware
4. 'Ee, Dunna Worrit'
5. Stop That Singing!
6. Sweeping the Bench Clean
7. Leaf and Blossom
8. Boneshakers and Sandcastles
9. Radio Days
10. Taking the Plunge
11. Through the Ranks

1. THE MUSICAL BLACKSMITHS

It's Sunday afternoon again. We've given the woods a miss, and we're off to the park. The band's playing and we intend to take a seat as close to the action as possible.

The bandstand faces a straggle of brass-lovers taking their places before the podium. The sun's out and hot, and the benches, in their crescent of shade, are nearly all occupied. We squeeze in as the uniformed bandsmen step up, testing their valves and make joking asides to ward off pre-performance nerves.

On the small pond behind us, unconcerned boys float their yachts and on the boating lake anglers check their floats. Rowers row, swans glide, strollers stroll, their voices distant in the heat-burnished air. The flower beds glow - salvia and marigold, petunia and rose, a mingled scent drifting across an enclosure of Sunday-scrubbed miners and their print-frocked wives. Jacqueline is asleep under the push-chair's awning; Michael's off to see the boats; my mother exchanges a word with the woman on the next bench and dad sticks his tie into his pocket.

'Well, it's very nice to be here again in Tunstall Park on this beautiful afternoon.' The conductor's voice floats on the air and a hush falls on the audience. 'We've a grand selection for you today, which I'm sure you're going to enjoy. That is, if I can get the band to stay awake. And so, without further ado, we'll start with that well-loved piece from *The Desert Song - One Alone.*'

'Oo, I like that,' coos my mother as the band prepares to strike up. 'That's one of my favourites.'

The baton is raised, the notes fall over lawn and playground, pond and lake, Floral Hall and bowling green, and in the still summer air can no doubt be heard by Father Ryan in his presbytery. The strollers are no longer as alone as the music suggests, for now their personal soundtrack accompanies them past the pavilion. Some are mouthing the closing words as the band, *rallentando*, nears the end: *This would be, a magic world to me, if she were mine alone....*

'Thank you ladies and gentlemen, the band always appreciates a good clap. It stops them falling asleep.' Titters from the audience. 'D'you know, I thought I caught a glimpse of the Red Shadow under the trees, but it must have been a trick of the light.' More laughter. 'Enough frivolity. Next we have a march by that famous American composer, Sousa. It's marching time with *The Stars and Strips for Ever.*'

'I don't think I know that one,' says mum

A feast of popular classics, hymns, overtures, operettas, arias, folk songs, show songs and anything else the conductor can lay his hands on is spread before the untiring audience, which has now swollen to incorporate passers-by, courting couples and youths bent on mischief. Gilbert and Sullivan's *Take a Pair of Sparkling Eyes* gets my father into singing mode, and my mother nudges him to keep quiet. Ivor Novello's *Rose of England* follows, and is followed by Tchaikowsky's *Skaters' Waltz*, Dvorak's *Humouresque* and Rossini's *William Tell Overture.*

The bandleader steps up to announce the final offering as the hat is passed around.

'Thank you for your generosity, ladies and gentlemen - and for bearing with me while the band practises. We'd like to bring this concert to a close with an old favourite of mine - and yours too, I hope - the famous Anvil Chorus from Verdi's *Il Trovatore.*'

'I think I know that one,' says mum. 'I think I heard it the other week on Family Favourites.'

Little girls thread daisy chains, a man slumbers beneath a knotted handkerchief, dad removes his jacket and rolls up his sleeves, Michael's mated up with a boy with a toy yacht and I'm listening to someone called Verdi, I think.

It's the blacksmith's hammer, wielded *marcato* which has a mesmeric effect upon three youths who've been cavorting on the boats. They now approach the bandstand to check out the elusive anvils. The band is fully into its stride, the bass drum pounding the hammer beat, an answering blast from the brass.

What the bandleader hasn't bargained for is the inclusion of the three new members who at this moment are peering through the balustrade and up his bandsmens' trouser-legs. Borne on a wave of nostalgia for the beat of the smithy's forge, they attempt an interpretation of their own.

The bass drum booms, the youths drop like ballet-dancers at the bar; and up again in time to the beat. Or at least one of the beats, since each is out of step with the other and both with either drum or band. It's only the increasing mirth of the audience, which is now laughing out loud, that draws the conductor's attention to his new recruits. A man of humour as well as musical ability, he now has the chance to conduct both band and jokers until the end is in sight and his unlikely converts beat a hasty retreat in the direction of Victoria Park Road.

A cloud passes across the sun, the band's already packing away, the man with the knotted handkerchief opens his eyes, my brother appears and makes a request for a yacht of his own. The audience drifts towards Tunstall or Chell, or stays for a walk, the park keeper's calling in a boat and my dad's calling to Michael to get down from the podium.

Tomorrow I'll be back in my Nissen hut at Chell, the band forgotten, the next visit to the park put on the back burner until another sunny Sunday, when the band will be entertaining us again.

2. TEMPLES OF DELIGHT

While Mr Bowers was finding out about his new arrival, the new arrival had found more pressing matters to attend to. Along with my next second-hand bike and trips to the woods and park, Barber's Picture Palace and the Ritz both made it to the list.

To me, the world of celluloid was one of delight and wonder. The magic began under Barber's art-deco cloisters, where we joined the queue for the early evening show. Particularly poignant was late autumn, when the days drew in and those shadowy figures shuffled in their best under the mist-swirling lights towards the entrance.

The cinema and its adjacent café seemed conspicuously out of place amid the worthy buildings ranked along Station Road. The Railway Station, Ryan Hall, the imposing Jubilee Buildings and the Market Hall all bore the confident stamp of their Victorian planners. Barber's was significant in its uniqueness; its glamorous façade announced itself in uncompromising terms. It was an interloper in a world of pit heaps and shraff tips, pot banks and marl holes, bottle ovens and saggars. Once the music crackled and the curtains parted, the townscape tumbled into a dusky netherworld and unreality became the new reality.

Wonderland needed its props too, and the commissionaire, as gaudily braided as an Argentinian *Coronel*, was our first link with the world behind the door.

'There's a double at the back and a single near the front.'

Our man was not inured to comments from the crowd, particularly during a cold snap when the pottery girls were losing the battle to keep warm.

'It's alright for you in your coat, I'm starved to death out here. It's freezing.'

'What's up, duck? Dunna thee run to a length o' melton down your street?'

'Who's running to Milton?'

'You're too nesh, that's your trouble. I'll see if I canna get you a couple o' braziers set up.'

'Don't be personal.'

You passed into the warmth of the foyer, and the girl in the kiosk handed you a disc as token of payment, to be produced and collected at the door of the auditorium. And auditorium dark was like no other, an intimate comfort-zone streaked with torch-light and rattling with pop-corn. It was here the gods of the silver screen would descend among us. Kathleen Hepburn and Spencer Tracy; Humphrey Boggart and Claude Rains; James Cagney and James Mason; David Niven and Merle Oberon; Gregory Peck, Errol Flynn, Cary Grant and Googi Withers: charismatic, tough, funny, beautiful or busty, these were the sort of people you'd never find at the bacon slicer or searching for a Penguin paperback in the Market Hall. They'd transcended all that. Such was their apotheosis, they could make you laugh or reach for you handkerchief, love or hate. Those flickering figures had our emotions by the short and curlies. You couldn't escape.

I must have been a morbid child, for it's the scenes associated with a calamity of some sort - usually death - that linger in my mind. Cornel Wilde's consumptive Chopin, coughing blood over the piano keys; Mrs Danvers leaping to her doom from the burning Mandalay; brooding Heathcliffe grabbing Cathy's ghostly hand at the open window; the old stag dying in the blazing forest; Snow White, pale, in her glass coffin. And when satisfying deaths were in short supply, I had to make do with the next best thing, death-free misery in black and white - *It Only Rains on Sunday* a promising example.

The Chums' Club only went in for tongue-in-cheek disaster. The venue this time was Tunstall Ritz, a faded temple of delights whose cavernous interior could easily swallow the crowds of ragged-trousered devotees with their shorn cox-combs and spud-heeled socks whose parents had forked out 6d to get them out of their hair for a couple of hours on a Saturday morning.

We were an exuberant bunch, brimming with brio and primed to cheer the moment the projectionist finished his Park Drive. The curtains parted, the screen lit and the gang greeted Donald Duck or Mickey Mouse with the telepathic arousal of the Port Vale crowd. Exaggerated bursts of laughter followed Mickey's every move, funny or not; wild yelps accompanied the rolling credits.

Other features produced a similar result. Abbott and Costello, Old Mother Riley and George Formby played to the undiscerning audience with equal success, our expectant faces lit by the glowing screen, the tin badges pinned to our jerseys by 'Uncle Bob' token of our membership of this exclusive club.

Next the serial, an intrigue involving one villain or another and, at the end, a cliff-hanging death for the hero who showed up in good health the following week after a miraculous deliverance. Failing that, 'Kagags and Injuns', the main contestants Hopalong Cassidy or the Cisco Kid - two suspiciously single forty somethings whose means of support remained unresolved, (unless it was a truss)

'Flash takes aim'

'Another fine mess.'

but who had time enough to chase baddies across the butte-scarred prairie just off Tunstall High Street. The Cisco Kid was also an early example of racial harmony, his smiling Native-American, Tonto, no doubt a step behind his boss at the Labour Exchange when the number of available baddies dwindled.

Happy, unquestioning days, the shared intimacy of my treks to the local cinemas some compensation for the shortcomings of the Home Service, where faces and locations had to be imagined and a bloke with a plywood panel supplied the thunder.

Though the Ritz has survived (not as a cinema), a block of flats now occupies the site of Barber's Picture Palace. The queues have gone, together with the commissionaire, the torchlight and popcorn. And those mist-swirling lights that announced your brief visit to wonderland.

3. STAINED GLASS AND BRASSWARE

My father's Sunday excursions ended at St Mary's Church, followed by a visit to my grandparents' house a hundred yards away. It was expected that my brother and I go along too, and we made the journey on foot from Chell Heath via Victoria Park Road, and Station Road, across the Square and down to Lime Street. A faint clamour of bells announced the Day of Rest. The traffic was still, the pavements deserted, the pot banks closed, the Loop Line silent.

St Mary's was impressive. It rose spectacularly from the surrounding terraces, its steeple both beacon and landmark. Had it been a person, rather than a cathedral in miniature, it could have been a big brother, upholder of my moral code but with a hint of menace and probably running a protection racket. It provided a conclusion to Lime Street and the other streets which radiated from it and which were unexpectedly curtailed at their western edge by the slopes of wasteland merging into Bradwell Wood. Austere, windswept, perched like a griffin above kilns, houses, shacks and marl-holes, it accepted its parishioners ungrudgingly as they trickled through its iron gates and along the path to take their habitual pew.

As with other large Victorian churches built for newcomers thrown up by the Industrial Revolution, the authorities had overlooked the problem of maintenance. Past its heyday even in the early Fifties, a decade later it was apparent that shrinking congregations could no longer look after it. The demolition of the terraces which served it was to prove its death knell. But I was too untroubled by future developments then, including my own. As far as I was concerned St Mary's was there for good, part of the weekly jig-saw which comprised my life.

The closing door was the prelude to prayer and contemplation before Vicar Cornes inaugurated the service. I was never sure whether the closed door was to shut the congregation in or to keep the rest of the world out. Whatever the truth, it had an inescapable finality to it. I was as helplessly imprisoned as the occupants of the other pews as *Jesu Joy of Man's Desiring* embalmed us in the tranquillity of spiritual reflection.

The organ did little to calm my own reflections, however, which came in red. My eye was particularly drawn to the swirling blood-red robes of the saints who lived in the stained glass, each with a golden nimbus and flowing

Pre-Raphaelite tresses which marked them out from the Lime Street bunch beyond the door. On bright days puddles of colour would stain the nave floor, the blue, green, gold and vermilion tints a dilute echo of those in the windows above. The church brassware, too, was polished to a high sheen; crosses and candle-holders, the sacred and secular, buffed to a winking Sunday gloss.

Into this world of vivid imagery came pairs of surpliced choristers, a leading member bearing the high cross, Vicar Cornes at the rear in vestments as richly embroidered as those of the saints above his head. The service had begun, the first hymn called, sung and ended, its words, red as the stained windows, filling me with an unintended sense of trepidation which made me shuffle nervously behind my hymnal.

> *Lift up Thy bleeding hand, O Lord;*
> *Unseal that cleansing tide;*
> *We have no shelter from our sin,*
> *But in Thy wounded side*

I was unable to resist these unwelcome images, which seemed to drizzle through the air. Apart from 'sin', which cropped up a lot, I wasn't sure what it all meant. But it meant something, and the something felt claustrophobic and unsettling. And when the hymn was over the saints continued to stare down at me from their sequined sky, just to make sure I was still on-message.

St Mary's was High Church, and few came higher than Vicar Cornes, a dark-haired ascetic attached equally to the swinging of incense and his non-swinging congregation. I once ran into him taking a short cut down Pickle Onion Entry and he didn't recognise me, so trivial was my part in the scheme of things. The Book of Common Prayer was his joy and scholarship, the creed sung to Hebraic cadences remembered to this day: *I believe in one God/Father Almighty, Maker of Heaven and Earth/ And of all things visible and invisible....*

St Mary's was not only a Sunday destination, with free entertainment and awe thrown in; it was part of the glue which cemented the weekly cycle, a place of pilgrimage, gossip and delight, where the hymns of Wesley, Newton, Lyte, Watts and Cowper were stairways to Heaven remembered long after the streets from which the congregations were drawn and the church itself had been reduced to hardcore.

When in 1954 my grandfather lay in an open coffin under the parlour window, it was in the sure knowledge he'd soon be borne through St Mary's gates, past the figure of the crucified Christ, down the old brick path and into the nave where he'd given away his daughters in marriage. Over twenty years later, when my grandmother followed him into that silent land she never doubted, the church had gone.

She was as lively as a cricket almost until the day she died. An intelligent woman whose life had been prescribed by chance and proscribed by lack of opportunity, she was nevertheless content with her lot and anxious to please. It seemed to me then, as it seems to me now, that my grandmother's joy was in service to others, her small daily kindnesses her stock-in-trade, her epitaph and the epitaph of her time.

I suppose that was her nature. But I'm sure St Mary's helped.

'Delight and gossip' - St. Mary's Tunstall.
Next door is St. Mary's Secondary School which I attended in 1951.

4 'EE, DUNNA WORRIT'

There was always a Sunday crowd at my grandparents house after church. The parlour was thrown open, the rarely-used chairs occupied, the display cabinet raided and the best cups passed around. My grandfather was disconnected from it all, and stayed put with his pipe in the living room.

Where this gathering came from, I don't know. They weren't from the local streets, and I doubt they were from Tunstall. One of their number was rumoured to have a Rolls Royce, and all fell into that category of the then church-going Middle Class, as defined by their scrubbed appearance, optimistic outlook and accents more BBC than Lime Street.

My grandma had a healthy regard for deference, and church and church people came near the top of her list. When they'd gone for another week, she was once more mistress of her domain, attending to her whittled down Sunday chores and my grandfather in equal measure, keeping up a steady dialogue with herself amid the rustle of coal and the rattle of crockery while he tamped the bowl of his pipe and read the Sunday paper.

He rarely spoke, and the little he did say was delivered in a Potteries' dialect which lingers in the speech of some older people, but which has largely been replaced in the young by the prêt a porter English of their television contemporaries. Grandma, on the other hand, was no slouch when it came to the local vernacular. Her stock of aphorisms was as well-worn as old shoes and kept for commonplace occasions which didn't include the Church crowd, where a less parochial language was called for.

She exhorted me to 'eat like a Christian', to 'behave like a Christian', to understand that 'cleanliness is next to Godliness', so I'd better wash behind my ears 'like a Christian' too.

She also had secular demands, and I was not the only target of them. My grandfather was cajoled to 'clean ite th' ess 'ole, (get rid of the ash from the grate) my brother told 'not to be nesh', (sensitive) and my father to 'wrap up warm 'less yer catch yer death'. Her advice was well intentioned, a drawn *ee* her sole exclamation, particularly when dealing with my grandfather:

'What's that on th' rug, Ginny?'
'What at talkin' abite, mon?'
'That theer, on th' best bit o' carpet'
'My, yer must 'ave good eyesight, ah canna see owt.'

'That o'er theer. All o'er th' rug.'

'Ee, it's only a bit o' dust ite o' th' grate'

'What's it doin' on th' best bit o' rug?'

'Ee. Dunna worrit abite it. Crumbs! If it bothers thee that much, I'll get thee a rag.'

Grandad would puff on his pipe, Grandma would bustle in with the food.

'An thee gone yet, Ginny?'

'Gone yet? Who?'

'Them as was 'ere a bit back, an thee gone?'

'Ee, they'n bin gone 'ayf an 'our sin'. Eat thee snappin' and stop goin' on abite it.'

'Ah dunna know why thee 'ast ow them folk round 'ere of a Sunday. Why canna thee go back wom like everybody else?'

'I've told yer, thee're friends o' th'vicar. Ah dunna know why yer keep on abite it every wick-end. They anna bin 'ere more than ayf an 'our at th'outside. I'm goin' across th' road, see 'ow tha George is goin' on....'

I was witness to their exchanges more than once, sitting on the chaise longue under the wall clock. Elderly then, their children long since flown, such daily skirmishes kept them both in full working order. They'd long since worked out their roles and stuck to them through thick and thin, sickness and health, slump and lay-off, childbirth and war, the last of the lumbering drays and the first of the clanking buses.

When they married five years before the Great War, my grandfather had been 32, his bride 17. He was the first to go, and after sixty years of marriage she sat bereft at his coffin in the parlour where she'd made guests welcome, dusted her few ornaments, displayed her china and peered down the street through the nets.

She remained sitting in her pew during the service, but rallied and survived. She went to live with her younger daughter and her husband, shortly to be the Reverend Percy Elliot Booth. The street where she'd lived since 1914 was bulldozed away in the Sixties, but by then she was bustling around vicarages in St Martin's, near the Welsh border, then at Silverdale, where Elliott had become the Parish Priest.

She bustled to the end, making tea for visitors, offering help, advice, and opinion whether sought or not, answering the door to anyone who wanted 'a word with the vicar'. She lived for the day, and if she harked back to her past, it was in private. Once, she told me she remembered the Tunstall crowds in mourning over the death of Queen Victoria, but she didn't elaborate, and I didn't probe.

When she died in 1976, aged 84, her era had drawn to a close - at least, as far as our family was concerned. The church which had been her mainstay and the street which had provided the narrative for her life had passed away with her, and the old Potteries dialect wasn't far behind.

She'd have taken it all in her stride, and if my grandfather had protested, she would have had her answer ready: 'Ee, dunna worrit abite it. If it bothers thee that much, do someat abite it an' join th'council.'

Gran and Grandad Ridgway at Lime Street, late 1920s.

5. STOP THAT SINGING!

Our Nissen huts at Chell weren't equipped for music or woodwork, so we had to use a two-room prefab built on the road-side slope of Chell Primary School. One accommodated a piano, the other lines of woodwork benches.

Our music teacher was Mr Abson, memorable at the time because of a growth on his neck rather like a hard boil. Just as Polly had seemed incomplete without his lurching larynx, Mr Abson and his spot were an item, like Fred Astaire and Ginger Rogers. He'd also attracted an addition to his name: Curly. Only on learning that Curly was bald did the nickname acquire its intended irony.

Curly's other legendary appendage was a large pump, which he would bring down on recalcitrant bottoms in flashes of anger which were by no means rare. Making a half-hearted attempt to sing *Men of Harlech* while keeping a weather-eye open for a change in mood could be a fraught business. The problem lay not only with a subject devoid of the constraints of formal lessons like table-practice, nor with the teacher or the songs he chose; it lay in all three, and we came to look forward to our weekly music lesson with an enthusiasm normally reserved for Light Programme treats like ITMA.

Curly had an inkling of what lay in store from the first batterings on his door.

'Can we come in, sir?'

'Stay out until I tell you. And stop banging the door. It's not there for your benefit. Wait outside till I'm ready.'

'But, sir -'

'Keep out. And leave the door shut and don't open it till I'm ready.'

'When will that be, sir?'

'WAIT OUTSIDE UNTIL I'M READY. THAT DOOR'S NOT THERE FOR YOUR BENEFIT!' Unimpeded by a range of inconsistencies presidential in ambition, he'd continue: 'And stop barging up against the wall, stand up straight and get off the wall!'

By this time he'd wrested his eye from the tattered score on the piano lid and, as the battering and barging continued, reached down for what might have been a Colt 45. It turned out to be the pump instead.

'What're we singing today, sir?' a voice called out, unfazed as yet by the gathering storm. 'Are we going to have something good this week?'

'Can we have *Coming Round the Mountain When She Comes*, sir?'

'No, sir, *Sweet Polly Oliver*, sir.'

'We had that last week. Sing *Annie Laurie*. I know the words to that.'

'I don't.'

'Sir! Sir! *The Ash Tree*, sir! Let's sing that.'

'It's not a nature study lesson. Line up and shut up! It's like a bear garden in here. I can hardly hear myself think.'

'Sir! Sir! *Barbara Ellen*, sir.'

'I know - *What Shall We Do With the Drunken Sailor*?'

An approximation was attempted by some of the bolder souls, drunken sailors taking the stage alongside Barbara Ellen, Polly Oliver and other unidentifiable characters who hadn't made it into Curly's hit parade. The contest was eventually won by *What Shall We Do With the Drunken Sailor*. Curly was unimpressed.

'Never mind what'll they do with the drunken sailor. I'll do something with *you* in a minute. Stop that singing! This is a music lesson, not a submarine. Who's still singing?' The raised pump now on standby, we were allowed in. 'Sit. Open your songbooks at Page 36: *Dashing Away with the Smoothing Iron*.'

A chorus of disapproval.

'The next one who calls out will get a dose of this!' The familiar artillery exploded on the piano lid. 'Alright! We'll learn a new song. Page 78: *The British Grenadiers*.'

There followed a flurry of turning pages, British Engineers sought as a substitute for the unrecognisable title. A pulse on Curly's neck seemed to throb, his fingers fighting the introductory chords as the early-warning system, like his face, went on red alert.

'How's it go, sir?'

'Sing it for us, sir.'

'I'M NOT HERE FOR SINGING! I'll say the words, follow them in your books:

Some talk of Alexander, and some of Hercules;
Of Hector and Lysander, and such great names as these;
But of all the world's brave heroes, there's none that can compare
With a tow, row, row, row, row, row, row for the British Grenadiers

'What a row, sir.'

'Please, sir, what's a grenadier?'

'He's nothing to do with it. Say the words.'

Songs of a military bent could usually be relied upon to elicit a variety of instrumental effects from the musical devotees facing Curly's soundboard. Once a week Polly Oliver would enlist as a soldier, hose pipes would be turned on the drunken sailor and gallant knights win their spurs in the stories of old. All this was as nothing compared to the patriotic fervour induced by *The British Grenadiers*. The lines had scarcely left Mr Abson's lips before the entire class, now transformed into a military band, was on its feet and ta-raring up and down room.

So intent was the trombone section, the approaching surge went unheeded and the dam broke, catapulting Curly and his pump into the melee, where various grenadiers were put to flight, leaving the rest to review their choice of an army career.

'Right, we'll have *The Ash Grove* instead. IF NO ONE HAS ANY OBJECTIONS. Now turn to it and the next one I find singing will get a double dose of this.'

So we did - or didn't, as the case may be.

6. SWEEPING THE BENCH CLEAN

Mr Toft was our woodwork teacher, his lessons delivered from the classroom next to Mr Abson's but within earshot of Polly Oliver and the swinging pump. Mr Toft was neither bald nor musical, and taught us how to make a trawler from a well-sanded length of three by one and an ambitious towel roller which could revolve on a dowel peg.

He wore horn-rimmed glasses and, clad in a brown overall, reminded me of a High Street grocer. A thick, carpenter's pencil protruded from his breast pocket, while his side pockets were burdened with screws, nails, pincers and a folding rule, together with most other items that could be found in a basic woodwork kit. These always accompanied him on his frequent tours between benches. I even saw a mallet stuck in there once. Without these props to his economic survival, he'd have felt somehow impoverished, like a trawler without a stack, or Curly without his grenadiers.

A pot of woodworking glue, whittled to a fraction of its former capacity by layers of treacly encrustations, bubbled under the steel-framed window. This was Mr Toft's favoured location on the rare occasions when he was stationary. He'd also attempted to make his section of the prefab look more academic, with wall charts showing schematic drawings of a dovetail, a mortise and tenon and a half-housing joint. The room smelled of sawdust and shellac, glue and shavings. He probably no longer noticed. He had his eyes on his charges, and we did things his way or not at all.

We were shown how to fashion our joints using chisel, template, mallet, and tenon saw, and told what jobs these joints were designed to do. Examples were demonstrated, elementary constructions attempted, the procedure for boiling glue spelt out, safety tips given and reinforced with the edge of a ruler if not followed to the letter. Over the year, most of us produced not only the trawler and towel roller, but a stool too, whether we wanted one or not. The trawler's funnel was a length of doweling glued into a hole, which introduced us to the drill; the towel roller's ends were attached to a rudimentary frame using dovetails, so we learnt how to use template and chisel, while the stool required mortise and tenon joints to connect struts to legs, so we learnt how to make those without splitting the wood.

'Gather around, boys. Form a circle.' We make an arc around the bench, looking like conspirators from the Gun Powder Plot. Mr Toft opens the doors at the end to reveal a set of woodworking tools. 'This is what you have in each bench. What did I say?'

'This is what you have in each bench, sir.'

'Name them.'

'A plane, sir-'

'Name them without looking.'

A collaborative effort eventually yields results.

'Next time you won't have to think about it.' He lifts the tools out one by one and places them on the bench. 'Now, then: what's this?'

'A chisel, sir.'

'One inch or half an inch?'

'One inch, sir.'

'And this - what's this part called?'

'The bevelled edge, sir.'

'Why don't we touch the bevelled edge?'

'Because you get cut.'

'Haven't you forgotten something?'

'Because you get cut - sir.'

'That's better. Now you can show me how you hold it.'

The chisel is passed around, and eventually someone gets it right. Mr Toft takes up the tools one by one and a brief talk follows: purpose, method of use, taking care of the tool, taking care you don't get hurt. Outside it's a grey November day and it's nearly four o'clock. The nights are drawing in and the strip lights inside the shellac-scented room are buzzing.

'Right, boys, it's nearly time for the bell. What d'you call this, Crofty?'

'A brush, sir.'

'It's a bench brush. Just like some of you lot, soft as a brush.'

The bell sounds faintly from the nearby Primary school. We're getting restless, and Mr Toft shoots a warning glance over his tortoiseshells. 'And when do we use the brush?'

Chorus: 'To tidy up at the end of a lesson, sir.'

'Right, sweep up. I don't want to see any shavings or sawdust. I want this floor so I can eat my dinner off it.'

A flurry of activity. The lights blink, the traffic hums behind the sawdust-webbed panes, Mr Toft busies himself by the glue pot. We do the job and stand by the benches, two to a bench.

'Finished, lads? Let's take a look.'

He inspects the rows and floor with nailbiting slowness. Like race horses too long stabled, we want to be off. And he knows it.

'There's a couple of specks by your bench, Smithy. Get rid of them.'

Smithy does.

'Right.' Pause. 'Ready to go?'

'Yes, sir!'

'Then -' Longer pause. 'What's that under your leg, Jonesy?'

Jones looks intently at the floor, the rest following with their eyes.

'I can't see nothing, sir.'

'I can. It's your shoe.'

Jonesy looks initially puzzled, but one by one they get the joke and he laughs along with the rest .

'Alright, you can go. See you again this time next week. And get your aprons washed.'

We've escaped. The mist has crept up from Tunstall, and I run through it all the way home. My towel roller only needs varnishing, then it's finished and I can screw it to the kitchen door.

Where it remains until the door is replaced thirty years later.

7. LEAF AND BLOSSOM

My grandparents' house not only accommodated the usual Sunday crowd; my father, my brother and I were expected to put in an appearance too. At the time Michael was a choirboy at St Mary's, which as far as my grandmother was concerned was a step up the ladder and a passport to better things both in this life and the next. I had no voice and no ambition in that direction, so I kept my head down and if a post-church dandelion and burdock was on offer, I drank it while the others partied. The crowd didn't take long to disperse, and then it was time for our walk to Bradwell Wood.

Memory is a law unto itself, storing and discarding at will. I remember no excursions to the wood in winter, though I'm sure they happened. Sharp in my mind are our walks in late spring, when a mist of bluebells brought a fresh palette to the sun-patched remnants of woodland. We took bunches back home to my mother by way of appeasement, because she'd been getting a late dinner ready while we'd been out enjoying ourselves.

Their musk fragrance delighted the air, as a gathered bunch would delight our kitchen window - and she wouldn't have come anyway. Ours was the innocent vandalism of another time, the wrath of the law then less confined to the activities of flower-pickers than to catching crooks. Neither did I have my collar felt for half-inching the campion which grew in unruly drifts amid hawsers and hawthorn.

For Bradwell Wood was unsure of its identity. Two centuries of pits and marl holes, bricks and tiles, had intruded into this part of the ancient Forest of Lyme, but had not wrecked it entirely. Discarded tips were less numerous than the stunted trees which found a root-hold in them; the remnants of buildings whose former use had been forgotten vied with abandoned clay quarries, shraff-tips, culverts, undismantled railway tracks, paths of broken tile and pitcher, nettle and willow herb, birch and alder, rills of rusty water and brakes burnished with buttercups.

The canal had been hacked from it, the railway thrust through. Tunstall had crept west and the A34 east. The last of the terraces jutted from its eastern edge and St Mary's spire spiked the clouds, with stacks and shacks competing for a place on the skyline. A scarp of dense woodland to the west filtered the noise of traffic, so that the sound of our footsteps was all we heard along the otherwise silent paths.

But enough of the wood had survived for the name to lack irony. In spring, tumbled masonry and discarded junk succumbed to leaf and blossom, willow herb and tansy, wood anemone and sorrel, the blackbird's chatter and the magpie's croak.

Pot-holed tracks and shard-strewn paths ran through these mysterious glades of bluebelled land. By May, the runnels were stippled with celandine and the screes with pussy-willow. In patches of mud marsh marigolds briefly flaunted their livery, frogs hid beneath an arabesque of roots and damsel flies flashed through patches of reed.

And it was here, in the pools of leaf-strained sunlight, that my father came into his own. The lethargy which too often gripped him at home was discarded as a spaniel shakes off water and he was off, my brother and me in tow, bounding through the green-girded wastes of his childhood as far as Peacock's Hey and Red Street, journey and purpose one.

It was at Peacock's Hey we discovered the first of many secret dells, its sides golden with gorse, the grass at its base manicured by rabbits and overseen by rooks. In September the briars were heavy with fruit, and my father found them with the assurance of a heat-seeking missile, using abandoned rabbit holes as toe-holds to lever himself up to the juiciest specimens. Tins were produced and quickly filled, later to be presented to my mother who, like us, had an appetite for blackberry pie.

A month later and it was time for mushrooms. Again, he never failed to track them down, their hiding places etched to his memory like the print of a dog's paw in a Roman tile. Perhaps he'd have been more suited to the life of a gamekeeper a generation before. He might have seen the Fifties as going places, and he didn't want to tag along. Perhaps he'd have been happier trapping rabbits and keeping an eye open for poachers than teaching at a local primary and thinking up ways to acquire his first car without going broke. Whatever the truth, our Sunday excursions made him forget himself, put the colour back in his cheeks, added a sparkle to his eyes and awakened a vitality that lay too often out of reach.

His was probably the last generation able to tell a coltsfoot from a daisy, a tree-creeper from a nut hatch and a toadstool from a mushroom; knew that rubbing a dock leaf on a nettle rash would take away the sting; ate hazel-nuts from the bush; knew that red clover was poisonous and white clover wasn't (because, he said, it reminded him of milk); relied on comfrey to treat a sprain; troubled to gather both feast and pharmacopoeia from that discarded half-land ten minutes from the park gates.

'Where've you been all this time? Your dinner's gone cold.'

'We brought you these, mum.'

'They look nice.'

'And these.'

'How many more tins have you got? No wonder you're late. There're no maggots in 'em, are there? Better put 'em in that bowl with some salt.'

'Can we have pie tonight?'

'I'll think about it.'

It came a day later, as it always did. But it was worth the wait.

A Sunday in Bradwell Wood. Me, Jacky and Mike.

8. BONESHAKERS AND SANDCASTLES

Most of our treats were modest. The *Beano* and *Dandy*, Charlie Kunz on the wireless and Sunday Roast in the oven; a blue bag of salt for your Friday crisps; Rupert Bear in the Daily Express; Ludo, Tiddly-Winks and Snakes and Ladders on the sideboard; the Hornby train-set I shared with my brother - along with a lace-up football and a cricket bat; Bayko houses and Airfix knights, balsa-wood planes and dinky toys. But some came specially packaged - our trip to London to see the Festival of Britain a case in point. This came somewhere near top of my treat list - and even that fell short of Rhyl.

I have a snap of the three of us there, my parents, brother and me, taken by one of those seaside photographers which, like the Mystery Man, were just beginning to eke out a living with their box cameras after the war. The finger of austerity still casts a shadow over the sunlit prom, my brother and me in underpants for want of a costume, my father in rolled-up sleeves and ill-fitting trousers, my mother wearing one of those belted print dresses which had to do, no matter what the occasion - a monochrome family straight out of the *Picture Post*.

That was in the late Forties, shortly before my sister was born. By the Fifties we had the trunks, and a towel to go with them. Things were looking up. Even so, my father was going through one of his debilitating attacks which kept him tethered to the war. Yet mine was a child's world, the trials of adulthood a closed shop to me. There was little to dampen our spirits and much to discover. Whatever problems my parents had to contend with they kept to themselves. Nor did the drabness of the town put me off, for it boasted one particular pleasure which my brother and I took advantage of: the cycle track.

About the same size as the playground where Mr Salmon had issued his marching orders, this hazardous oval could unwittingly have been the blueprint for subsequent Health and Safety legislation. A few coppers secured the bike of your choice, disentangled from a scree of cannibalised cycles parked against a wall.

My earlier brush with the tree at Peck Mill Lane may have been behind my decision to choose a trike, rather than the two-wheeler whose look-alike had given me trouble. Although the tricycle looked as if it had had a lucky escape from the breaker's yard, I wheeled it out. Rust speckled and almost brake-free, it and I joined an elite bunch of riders disdainful of petty refinements like fixed saddles and fully inflated tyres.

The only rule seemed to be that you pedalled frenziedly in a vaguely clockwise direction. Everything else was up for grabs, and since even those waiting for a free bike became unhinged once the wheels began to turn, the local hospital seemed as good a destination as any when your ten minutes was up. Fortunately, within a couple of grazes, we were flagged to the pit stop and we were off to the beach.

Visiting the beach without a bucket and spade was like bubble without the squeak. My brother's bucket, ready for the task in hand, was of brightly painted tin, his windmill of bright cellophane. Although I pretended to be too old to be bothered with such trivia, I couldn't wait to show him how it was done.

At the time, skilled sand-sculptors could be seen crafting horses and mermaids before an admiring audience. Despite this example of what could be achieved, bucket and spade productions never got much further than making a sand-castle, and not a very convincing one at that.

The routine was always the same: damp sand was shovelled into the bucket with a tin spade and flattened level with the rim. The bucket was inverted and whacked a couple of times before being slowly lifted to reveal a flat-topped cone. Recrimination was the consequence of an imperfect tower, the accuser insisting he'd make a better job of it given half a chance.

This invoked wrath: *'You're* not having a go. It's *my* bucket. Get off and buy your own. Mum! He's run off with my spade!'

Though some bucket-bangers got above themselves, creating multi-turreted forts and even venturing into two storey jobs, most opted for a simple tower surrounded by a moat. This was scooped out by the architect and his mate using shovel and hand, the work incomplete until enough water had been lugged to the site to afford the fort the desired level of impregnability. The windmill was stuck on top to bring the project to a satisfying conclusion. Failing that, a raised Union Jack would impart a dash of patriotism before the incoming tide washed away the lot.

There was no dedicated cycle track at New Brighton, nor do I recall us having to fortify the shore-line with our sand castles. It seemed hardly worth defending anyway, the same run-down post-war feel featuring here as at Rhyl and much of the Potteries. Municipal planting lent some relief, the plots in parks and proms laid out with displays of petunias, pansies and antirhinum, but such shows were rare enough to hold the attention of those who'd been obliged to make-do-and-mend and to whom frivolity was long overdue.

Why had my father decided on New Brighton? Who knows? As with his choice of ebony floors, soused herring, gorgonzola and bottle-green dados, he seemed to embrace a sepia seaside austerity. Our New Brighton guest house was part of this pattern. An indifferently furnished Victorian villa, the landlady prepared meals from food purchased by my mother which we ate alone in an uninviting dining room. I'm not sure how much my surroundings mattered at that time. They must have had some effect, since the description above is largely how I saw it as a child.

It didn't put my father off. We were dragged along to the wax works, where the chief exhibit was a man being mauled by a grizzly. To offset the nightmare this inevitably produced, the following night found us in a dowdy theatre where the male troupers, in top hats and suspenders, went through some comedy dance routine which coaxed a laugh from my father but didn't do much for the rest of the audience. At intervals throughout the early Fifties, when his health, though improving, suffered a set-back, he was prescribed a week's rest and New Brighton was where he took it.

Much of that post-war landscape has gone. The blocks of concrete laid along the beaches to deter German landing craft were disposed of long ago, the grizzly and its prey melted down, the cycles scrapped and the track they ran on redeveloped. And though sand castles are still holding out, the architect's plastic bucket has replaced the tin version. The kind of seedy guest houses we used at Rhyl and New Brighton have been replaced or modernised; the towns have long since had their make-overs.

The past, with its moods, sounds and colours, is another country. Things were different there. All the same, should the cycle track ever be reintroduced, I'm sure there'd be a new crop of enthusiasts ready to chance their arm. Or leg.

9. RADIO DAYS

Ben Mallinder sold bicycles and their accessories from his Tunstall shop. When I was in the High Street I'd gawp at the shining machines propped at a rakish angle to the door and wish I could own one of them, chromed to within an inch of its life and framed and forked in gleaming black. Some models even came with a Sturmey Archer three speed gear and a dynamo, as long as you paid the right price.

Ben had long since got used to the wealth of bright wheels in his care. His overall, probably purchased from the same shop visited by our woodwork teacher, bore the marks of his trade in tell-tale oil stains and rumpled pockets. Cycle repairs were carried out 'round the back' and out of sight of the showroom, so that the beat-up machines which came in to be mended wouldn't detract from the flashy magnificence of the latest models on display.

There was a faint tang of dust, oil and cardboard inside the store and a faint clang of traffic outside it. Ben didn't hang about, but was one of those shopkeepers who materialised at the ring of the bell. The shop seemed empty, you opened the door, the bell pinged and there he was, like a genie from a bottle - or in his case, from an oil can. He was polite, rather than deferential, and it seemed to me he wasn't too concerned whether you bought one of his bikes or not.

Ben had a sideline, which might have been mainline - accumulators. When we lived at Pinnox Street this intriguing cell, full of a clear liquid - we were told never to get on your skin because it burnt and was called acid - had to be taken along to Ben to 'charge up'. An accumulator was quite heavy, and it was down to my dad or uncle Lou to lug it up the High Street to Ben, where he'd exchange it for another which had already been charged. All this charging business was one of those magical rites adults went through when they wanted to listen to the wireless. I knew that the accumulator eventually 'ran out of charge' and when that happened the voices on the sideboard would begin to crackle and fade until Ben had worked his alchemy and we could tune in to Arthur Askey for another week.

The wireless at Sib's was a bulky affair which eclipsed the minstrel boy sharing the sideboard with it. It had seen better days, the fabric covering the speaker torn in places, the knobs loose, the glass panel bearing the names of exotic locations scratched and chipped. Even so, it was our gateway to a changing world and the focal point of the room. Manufactured before the local terraces had been coupled to the grid, Ben and his accumulators comprised the back-up team which kept us entertained, informed and amused throughout the winter nights.

By the time we moved to Chell Heath, the days of the accumulator had gone. The wall sockets supplied with our council house might have looked like Bakelite cocoa cans - and there weren't so many of them - but we had an electricity supply which propelled us into the modern age and my father went again to Ben Mallinder's, where he purchased a Bush.

Our Bush wireless was an ultra-modern, state-of-the-art receiver. More compact and more reliable than its predecessor, the need to charge the accumulator had passed into history, together with the indifferent sounds the old set produced. The Bush was a must-buy as far as my dad was concerned, and Ben passed it in its cardboard box over the counter with the sort of knowing look that suggested he was handling a technological breakthrough, and that by implication my father was a man of the moment who knew what was what and had the wherewithal to do something about it.

We caught the Bedford bus with the appliance secure on his knee. At home it was unwrapped with a reverence normally reserved for a bottle of Christmas whisky and carefully placed on the sideboard near to the mains socket. Never a man for the screwdriver, dad nevertheless procured a plug from somewhere and fixed it up. The knob was clicked to 'on', the dial lit, the volume gingerly increased. We had sound. Good sound. My father beamed and dared to tamper with the other knob, which gave us the Light Programme, the Home Service and a whole range of wonders which would keep us entertained for years to come. We might have a cobbler's last dating from the last century in the outhouse, and my mother was still using fire-warmed irons, but on the wireless front we weren't to be beaten. And it was only 1951.

Just as the accumulator wireless had taken pride of place on the sideboard at Sib's, so the Bush rivalled the fire as the centre-piece of our Chell Heath living room. A good programme was marked with a bottle of dandelion and burdock and a bag of crisps, the family gathered around the wireless as if it were a winter log.

We listened to home-grown products which were uncompromisingly British, the accent that of the clipped upper class and no light-hearted japes on a Sunday if you please. The Reithian charter - to educate, inform and entertain - was the guiding principal, and I took full advantage of the entertaining part. On Saturdays it was *Variety Night*, with Henry Hall and his band providing the music. Then there was Arthur Askey and Richard Murcoch's *Comedy*

Bandwagon, which, like Tommy Handley's ITMA, had played to war-time audiences and had lost none of its attractions. It was in ITMA that the character Mrs Mop came into her own, and we'd be ready for her catch phrase 'Shall I do you now, sir?' to produce a spontaneous laugh, though we didn't really know why we were laughing.

Other offerings kept us chuckling along: *Much Binding in the March, Ray's a Laugh, Take it From Here* and Arthur Askey's *Hello Playmates* each had their niche in the week's schedules. And when comedy wasn't on offer, Dick Barton drew me so convincingly into the world of espionage my dandelion and burdock remained unsipped and my crisps uneaten.

It was Radio Luxemburg, bursting into our homes in 1952, that threatened to topple the BBC from its perch. This new station was dangerous, elicit and seductive. Suddenly, the Home Service was for granddads in cardigans. Luxemburg gave a willing audience more of what they wanted, with Leslie Welch 'the famous memory man' and The Adventures of Dan Dare, Pilot of the Future later giving way to games shows like Hughie Green's Double Your Money and Bernard Miles' *Take Your Pick* - both of which later made it to television.

But whatever the fare, it had been supplied courtesy of Ben Mallinder's Tunstall shop, and things were never the same after that.

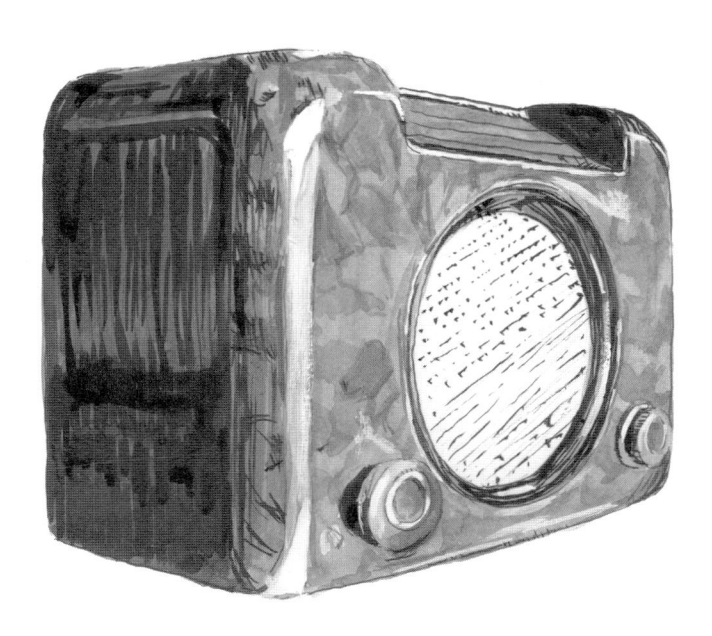

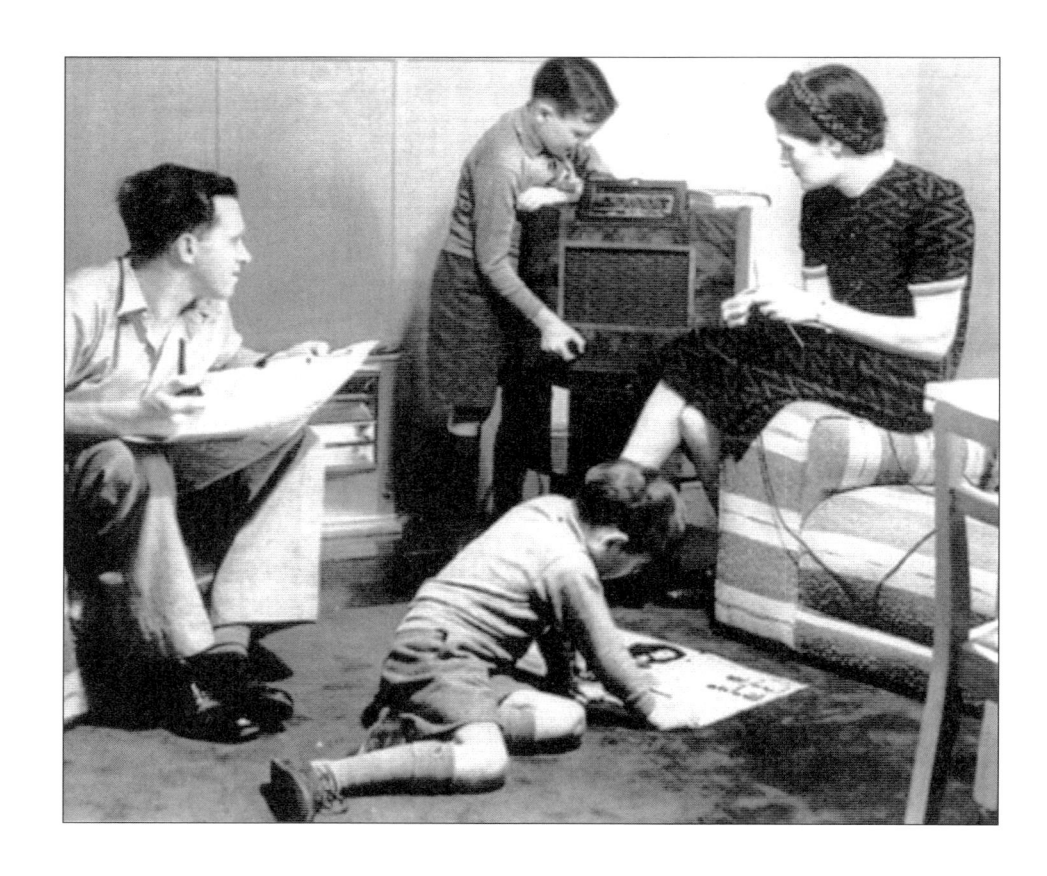

Tuning in, 1940s.

10. TAKING THE PLUNGE

Once a week we were marched from school to Tunstall Baths, where I learnt to swim. Tunstall Baths was part of a handsome block built by the city fathers in response to the rising demand for education and physical fitness. The provision of parks away from kiln and factory smoke fulfilled much the same purpose.

Baths of any kind were still a worthy destination in the early Fifties. The pool at Tunstall retained its ambience, the water a couple of feet lower than the side, the cubicles built to maintain Victorian modesty still with their doors and plank seating intact. An adjoining room catered for bathers from the surrounding terraces which lacked the luxury of bath or shower, and a small fee entitled them to the pleasure of a hot soak with soap provided.

My early attempts at the dog paddle bore fruit. Before long I'd mastered a couple of strokes and accomplished my first length without fanfare or certificate. Armed with a new confidence as well as a new hobby, I soon transported my modest skill to Burslem Baths at the week-end, where I became a pearl diver on the look out for pennies and tried my hand on the diving board with indifferent - and sometimes painful - results.

It didn't put me off. By this time I'd acquired another bike, similar to the machine which came to grief down Peck Mill Lane but with new brake blocks. Armed with two hobbies, swimming and cycling, my weekend destinations were already mapped out for me. I believe that as a twelve year old set on exploration, it was the scent of chlorine that guided my pedals for a couple of years.

Together with a swimming/cycling companion who lived nearby, I made a chlorine-free discovery one afternoon at Smallthorne. It had been a still, warm day and we had time to kill. By chance I spotted, through a gap, a ruined building I'd never noticed before. We decided to explore, and found ourselves in a tiled enclosure looking down on a pool long devoid of water. It was still tiled in parts, in places weeds had encroached, and around the side were the remains of cubicles. No one had ever spoken about a lido at Smallthorne before - it came as a surprise to find one there, engulfed by roads and the spoil heap of Sneyd Colliery.

I discovered later that it had been a victim of mining subsidence, like its art-deco companion at Trentham Gardens. It's doubtful whether it ever made a profit, but lidos were all the rage before the war, and on that afternoon we glimpsed an echo of its former glamour. We wondered what the potters and miners who lived round about would have made of it all.

Further watery adventures beckoned. We'd found out about another open-air pool close to Leek, and although at that age Leek was foreign parts, we decided it was about time we spread our wings. We'd already been as far as Knypersley, which was more or less on the road, and figured another few miles was neither here nor there.

With sandwiches, a shared Tizer, bathing trunks and towels stuffed into our saddlebags, we set off to find this elusive venue, which we now found had a name: Freshwater. Nearly two hours later, we turned off the Leek-Macclesfield road and headed up a track towards a glimpsed diving board and within earshot of the screams of those using it.

The pool was more a natural pond. A small range of sheds, one of which doubled as a changing room, overlooked a stretch of water crowded with bobbing heads and aquatic gymnasts. Shivering figures lay huddled and towelled on the surrounding grass. A few bikes were strewn in a corner, and we added ours to the pile and changed.

A toe in the water gave you a good idea of what lay in store, and why the pool was called Freshwater. This euphemism could have been substituted for any number of names which would have done a better job, most of which would have had to include 'freezing' at some point, together with 'ice' and 'exposure'. Perhaps it was this bracing characteristic which put the pool on the local map, the hardy swimmers who embraced it forgoing the milder waters of a municipal dip to prove they could swim in Freshwater and live to tell the tale.

From toe we progressed to midriff and after twenty minutes took the plunge. Glacial melt was tepid in comparison, and as the water knocked the air from our lungs and put my newly discovered crawl under severe restraint, I snatched a look at other masochists whose own grimaces did nothing to make me feel better. How long would I be able to stand our latest bright idea? Ten minutes? Fifteen? More would be pushing it, and we were out and rummaging for a towel in less than five.

We sat, shivering, on the grass. The sandwiches came out, we dried off, and despite the hot weather remained cool for the rest of our stay. Later excursions to open air pools at Market Drayton and, of course, Trentham Gardens, never had quite the impact of Freshwater. I still enjoy the occasional dip in the local leisure centre or hotel pool, but they're kids' stuff. If you really wanted to experience the hallucinatory effect of an Arctic winter, Freshwater was the place to be. It's a pity it's not still there, you'd not be disappointed. I promise you.

11. THROUGH THE RANKS

'You've done well, Ridgway. We're moving you to a higher group. When you come back next term you'll be in 1D. Mr Abson's class.'

It came as something of a surprise to discover that Mr Abson, that promoter of folk songs and summary justice, would shortly be sharing a hut with me. This time he put music on hold and opted to teach me English and History instead.

1D represented a step up the ladder, and I found myself competing with thirty-six others, some of whom were clever. By this time I'd learnt to be less blasé about success, and my varied school career began to suggest it might be a good idea if I played to win, rather than to simply take part. I was what they then called a 'late developer'. I'd come top in 1E not because of any great effort on my part, but because I'd been wrongly placed in a form where poor reading and writing was the norm.

I was a late developer not only academically, but in attitude too, content to coast along without putting in the extra pennyworth which would have given me greater confidence. An inchoate seed of ambition made itself felt. I began to wonder what the Hanley High School lads had that I hadn't. Why should they be treated to the biplane parked by the entrance in honour of ex-pupil Reginald Mitchell - and visible from Chell roundabout - and not me? Why wasn't I expected to carry a satchel too?

I did some pondering. While Johnnie Ray was walking his baby back home and Eddie Fisher was warbling *Wish You Were Here* I was wishing I was there. By the end of the Spring Term, 1952, I came ninth in class, and at the end of the Summer Term I'd moved four more notches up the greasy pole. At the same time Dr Gardner took over from Mr Marshall as Head. Whether this augured well I didn't know, but the word 'doctor' had the ring of status, and being stuck under an arch of corrugated steel while 'the others' learnt shove ha'penny and Latin - I wanted some of that.

I moved to 2D in the Autumn Term and a new form teacher, Mr Mellor, who now took us for English, French and Divinity. A pleasant, fair-minded man, he laid down the ground rules for the construction of sentences: ten spellings to be learnt by the end of the week and punctuation practice daily. His reward for latecomers - of whom I was once one - was a single and not very painful stroke of the cane. Now I was putting my back into my work;

even our square-jawed art teacher, Mr Morris, another of those firm but fair masters who were the mainstay of Secondary Schools in the Fifties, said so.

It was partly because of this unsought encouragement that I took the 13-Plus. By the Spring Term of 1953 I'd moved to third in my new class, and for the moment the gods of fortune were smiling on me. My routines became as familiar as Billy Cotton's *Wakey! Wakey!* and the smell of Sunday roast. The wail of the Riley Arms siren no longer brought back images of the war. A buoyancy reigned at home and out of it. The new monarch was on her way and we'd joined the High School in a crocodile to Barber's for a dose of celluloid patriotism, Everest was about to be climbed, the double-helix discovered, the band at Tunstall park would shortly find Teddy Boys, if not among the audience, at least practising their steps below the rostrum, my family were rubbing along. The only cloud on an otherwise sunny horizon was an accident at Chatterley Whitfield colliery which claimed the life of a friend of my father's. I believe the man's name was Hughes, and I recall my feeling of vicarious grief for his son, who was in the same class.

But I was young, my life a collection of fleeting moods and moments intruded upon by Guy Mitchell, Frankie Lane and Jo Stafford when I let them, and cycle rides out with a mate. The words of the song of the moment, *Jambalaya* were putting me off my stride when I heard Mr Mellor call us to attention. Would anyone who wished to take the 13-Plus examination please see him at the end of the lesson? The rest of the class gave a collective shrug and got on with the work in hand. I couldn't. I knew I had to take the examination, set up for people like me who'd failed the 11-Plus and might now have a better chance. At the end of the lesson I hung back.

'You want to be entered for the exam, Ridgway?'

'Yes, sir.'

'I'll put your name down.'

Mine shouldn't have been the only name on the list. At least one other classmate would have stood a better chance than me, had he put his name forward. He hadn't, so a month later I found myself alone in an empty office with a bottle of ink and a folded question paper. *Write an account in not more than 400 words of a recent scientific invention you consider of great importance. Give reasons for your choice. OR In not more than 400 words, outline a major problem facing the world today, and what steps you would take to overcome it.*

Recent? Major? Account? My mind blanked, then focused. Shaking off a swamping inadequacy, wondering what I was doing in that inquisitorial chamber while the bars of sun-light played across the floor, I took up my pen and began to write: *I think the artificial insemination of cattle is a great scientific advance. According to the wireless, many cows have not been able to give birth to a calf until now because....*

What a smug and pretentious weed I must have seemed to the examiners. What did I know of insemination, artificial or otherwise? How on earth had I latched on to the stream of garbled half-facts which now, in full spate, tumbled across the page? What did I know of a dalesman with a three foot syringe - a boy from a Stoke-on-Trent housing estate whose flights of fancy extended no further than Desperate Dan's cow pie? Why hadn't I stuck to penicillin or the jet engine, even had I known about either, than to enter the territory of reproductive economics? I left the office in that written-out state of exhausted calm which is sometimes mistaken for confidence.

Just as my memory of the 13-Plus, let alone any hope I had of passing it, was beginning to fade, I was sent for. This time I found myself in a different office - Dr Gardner's office, in fact, with Mr Marshall seated in a corner.

'Good morning, Ridgway.'

'Good morning, sir.'

'You've been busy taking the 13-Plus examination?'

Was I being asked to answer a question or corroborate a fact? 'Yes, sir.'

'Very well.' A half-smile played across his mouth. 'How's your Maths?'

'Alright, sir....not as good as English.'

Mr Marshall coughed in sympathy. Dr Gardner smiled non-commitally. I hoped they wouldn't get wind of the tense nervousness which had gripped my stomach and given my fingers a life of their own.

'If I brought twenty items and paid £2.19.6d for each, how much change would I receive from £60?'

Was it a trap? I struggled for an answer. 20 at £2.19.6d. Call it £3. That makes £60. Knock off twenty sixpences. How much is that, twenty sixpences? Ten shillings. What was the first figure? Sixty pounds? Yes, that was it. Take 10/- from £60....

'£59.10s, sir.'

'Are you sure you're not giving the total cost. You were asked for the change from £60.'

'Sorry, sir. Ten shillings, sir.'

'You got there at last.'

'Yes, sir.'

'Thank, you Ridgway. You may go back to your class.'

A week later I was called back to the Head's office. A feeling of trepidation dogged me as I walked past the Nissen huts and up the steps to the rear entrance to the High School. Behind the glass-walled corridors, rows of scholars had their heads bent over their texts, their gown-wearing masters studiously vacant behind their desks. I ticked off each echoing stride as I made my way along the corridors to the now familiar door and knocked.

The door stood ajar. 'Come in.' I eased it open. 'Ah, Ridgway. Sit down.'

'Yes, sir.'

'I have some pleasant news for you. You've gained a place at grammar school. Are you pleased?'

'Yes, sir.'

'Well done. You know the school's moving to Bucknall in September?'

'I think so, sir.'

'You've worked hard. You deserve your place. Has Mr Mellor told you you've come top of your form this term?'

'No, sir. Not yet, sir....have I?

'You can close the door on the way out.'

Only later did it sink in. I was to be one of *them*. But - was I up to it?

'Your father will be pleased,' my mother said when I got in. 'Get me a few carrots out, will you?'

But I was already in the back yard, bouncing a tennis ball off the shed wall. Maybe it was the artificial insemination that clinched it.

5. CHANGING TIMES

Two years into my time at Hanley High School would see the beginnings of a step change in the country. In the words of the Abba song, the Post War world was 'slipping through my fingers'. Youth was finding its feet, and its feet came with crepe-soled beetle-crushers and luminous socks. At the same time my grandfather's sister Annie still slopped the quarries in an ankle-length dress which wouldn't have been out of place before the Great War.

Our Bush would shortly be eclipsed by the slow-to-warm-up 12" television set my father had bought for the Coronation; Lita Roza by Elvis Prestley; the drab by the bright. The dump where we'd built our dens would be levelled and seeded for football pitches, the first second-hand cars bought by our neighbours and parked down the street. The winds of change were blowing.

But the old world still clung on. It would be a decade before Dr Beeching's accountants persuaded him the Loop Line would make more as scrap, and for now the Fowler tank engines' distinctive chuff-chuff could still be heard from my bedroom window on a still summer's evening as they left Pittshill Station.

Even with my nose pressed against Pepper's window and my covetous eye oggling the gleaming red MG TDs behind the pane, the rumble of Hanley traffic came mainly from the Morrises, Wolseleys and Austins built before the war. The latest gas-fired kilns hadn't yet ousted the bottle oven from the city skyline; a friend on the staff of J and G Meakin was still addressed as 'Master John' by potters who'd begun their working life in the deferential days of Edwardian Stoke; I took it for granted that the world was white - until, in 1958, I found vacational work at Doulton's, where I saw my first Asian.

Hanley High School fought its own battle with the times, the gowned masters expected to follow an academic curriculum rooted in a public school tradition while Lonnie Donnegan ignored them and rode the Rock Island Line instead.

The first eight articles in this final section are intended to reflect those changes, which swept us into the Swinging Sixties. These are followed by an interview I carried out with Eva Twigg, once Deputy Cashier at Tunstall Woolworth's - a store which crops up more than once in this book. The last chapters are adapted from two articles I wrote for *The Way We Were*.

Chapters

1. An Extra Nut

2. Sidetracked

3. Rebranding

4. Wielding the Willow

5. Shifting Sands

6. Cosines and Sideburns

7. Parted Curtains

8. Water Under the Bridge

9. A Life of Riley

10. A Bizarre Fortune

11. Mops, Socks and King Edwards

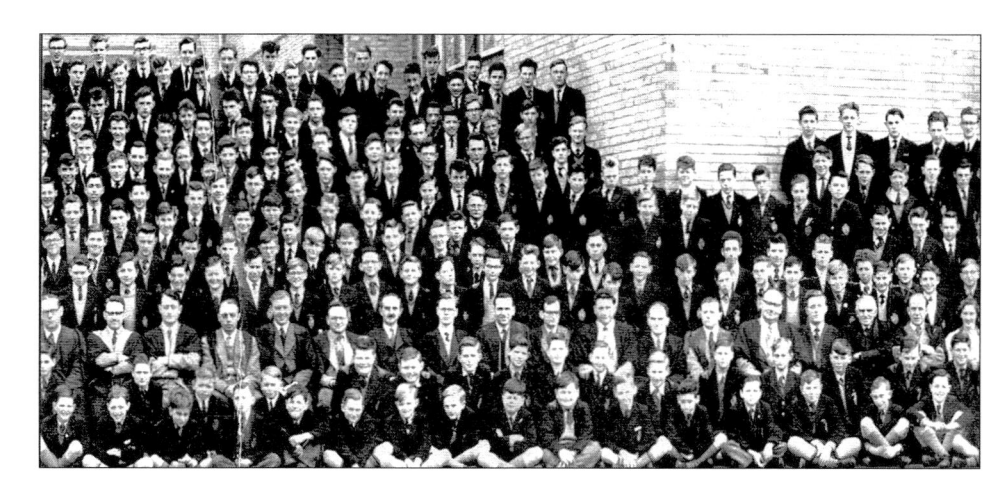

Masters and students - Hanley High School, 1956.

1. AN EXTRA NUT

During the long summer holiday after leaving Chell Secondary School, I thought I'd look for part-time work to supplement the weekly pocket-money I got from my father. Looking for a job at thirteen was a tall order, and I wondered how to go about it.

As luck would have it, a friend had managed some week-end employment packing and delivering orders for a grocer whose store was one of a handful of Chell Heath shops built to serve the estate. He said he'd put a word in with the boss for an assistant.

These premises seemed to change hands a lot, apart from the fish and chip shop, which always drew a crowd from the Knave of Clubs at kicking out time and rivalled the ice-cream van in its knack of drawing in the punters for a Friday night treat.

The grocer's had survived long enough for the locals to take advantage of the delivery service offered, and my friend had endured the tribulations of his errand-boys' bike long enough to ask for someone to help. Unexpectedly, the boss agreed.

This was a mixed blessing, since my companion was hoping to use his employer's anticipated refusal as a pretext to leave. Unfortunately, my arrival cemented the deal and after I'd been shown the ropes, the two of us settled to bag the orders. The bike-basket was then loaded with as few items as my friend could get away with before he set off on the round while I packed the next batch.

All was not well. The bike had seen better days, with consequent delays in delivery time despite the contents of the basket being whittled to the weight of a sugar bag. On his return, the grocer was waiting. He wasn't happy.

'What time d'you call this?'

'I had trouble with the bike. It's got a slow puncture. I had to lend somebody's pump.'

'You've always got a slow puncture. Have you done all your stops?'

'I only did one. I couldn't carry no more. This bike weighs a ton.'

'Weighs a ton? I could carry that lot on my head. You'll be making your last drop gone midnight at this rate. You'd better get your skates on and load up.'

His comments did nothing to encourage my friend's application to the job in hand, and by four o'clock there was still a sizeable pile of goods waiting to be delivered. By now I'd finished bagging up, and he looked aghast at the remaining work. At the same time he was cunning enough to draft me into the rest of the day's activities.

Besides the bike, a small hand-cart stood against the store room wall. Now he suggested I wheel out half the remaining groceries using this, while he continued with the bike as before. I was in no position to argue. We loaded up and set off.

The delivery service now began to acquire a competitive edge. The cart was heavy and cumbersome, the bike, steerable only if a modest walking speed was maintained. We were in sight of each other for much of our journey, and despite mis-directed items and absent customers, we were well on the way to clearing the backlog. It wouldn't be long before the 5 shillings ended up in my sticky palm, then I'd be off to Tunstall to find something to spend it on.

It was five and we'd almost finished when the front tyre of the delivery bike finally gave up the ghost. By chance, I finished my round - and he his - outside his house. Now he decided to fix the machine once and for all, and disappeared indoors for spanners and a puncture repair outfit.

It was getting late by the time we'd freed the wheel and prized off the tyre. Locating the puncture involved an ear cocked for the hiss of air, and when this proved ineffectual, a bucket of water. While all this was going on, I winkled from the junk in my pocket a nut similar in size to the wheel nuts and placed it on the pavement alongside them.

The inner-tube soon boasted a new patch to add to the twenty or so already decorating its circumference. A grating of chalk was applied and the tube tested.

'Is the rim OK?' I asked, injecting a note of innocent caution into my query.

'I've already checked that.'

'No spokes sticking out?'

'No, I've checked. I'm getting this tyre back on, then I'll get the bike back before he locks up.... you go on in front if you want and tell him I'll be down.'

His spanner was out and ready for the wheel.

'No, I'll wait for you,' I said, 'in case it goes down again.'

He was hand-tightening the wheel nuts when he caught sight of my own addition on the pavement. 'Where's that from?'

'What?'

'That nut? Where's it from?'

'Is it off the bike somewhere?'

A puzzled frown spread across his face as he hoisted the machine upright, moving it this way and that in a vain attempt to spot the place lacking the erratic nut, which was smirking at him from the pavement.

'I don't get it. Where's it from?'

After a futile struggle to hold a straight face, I came clean. He wasn't impressed. Neither was the grocer.

'D'you know it's gone six? I've been stood here like a lemon. Where have the pair of you been all this time?'

'I found the puncture,' my mate began, 'and he played a trick on me while I was fixing it.'

'Well, you can leave the bike round the back and the pair of you needn't bother coming back next week. I'll get someone who's up to the job.'

'What about my five bob?'

'I'm knocking off 6d for keeping me hanging about. Count yourself lucky I've not stopped the lot.'

Thus my first day of work ended soon after it began. And it was all my fault. Even so, my companion wasn't too put out. He didn't tell me at the time, but he'd already got another job lined up. As an errand boy at a butcher's. It meant an extra shilling a day.

And he'd be delivering - by bike.

2. SIDE-TRACKED

My aunt Anne had inherited a different set of genes to the rest of the Ridgways. My Celtic grandmother had bequeathed my father and his three other sisters her black hair and brown eyes and their cup was usually half empty. Anne, on the other hand, was fair, blue-eyed and resilient, and her cup always came half-full with the promise of an extra shot. Life, to my dad and his other sisters, had something lurking up its sleeve and you'd be wise to dodge out of the way before it got you; Anne was more likely to grab the coat by the lapel and put the boot in. She gave of her best, ignored the worst and got on with things.

She wasn't afraid of plunging in at the deep end, and tried her hand at a range of jobs before settling on a teaching career. While I was trundling my trolley around the estate, she was busy at Keen's, selling twin sets and womens' underwear. Keen's occupied an inconspicuous site at the end of an alley to the side of what was then the Midland Bank in Tunstall. It was a modest enterprise, but did a surprising amount of business in the Fifties.

No area of floor or shelving had been overlooked by the stockists, and on the rare occasions I was delegated to take a message to Anne 'at the shop' I found myself negotiating racks of nighties, hangers of blouses, shelves of packaged stockings and a range of other items labelled 'flannelette', 'winceyette' and 'sheer nylon' which augmented the basic wool and cotton goods on display. The volume of fabrics tended to deaden sound, so that a shout of 'Fire!' for example, would have gone unheard amid the drapes.

Anne worked her way up from counter assistant to buyer, from time to time appearing at my grandmother's house with expensive outfits at a knock-down price. She was good at her job - her next move to the library around the corner a source of regret to the manager, who'd come to depend on her business acumen.

The chains hadn't then intruded into Tunstall and towns like it, and many of the shops were owned by local businessmen and staffed by local women. Though Tunstall had its Woolworth's and Burton's, the really big stores - Lewis's, Marks' and Spencer's, British Home Stores - were confined to Hanley, the commercial hub, and the place serious shoppers went to when they fancied a Saturday out..

Hanley was still an exotic destination as far as I was concerned, and I rarely had the money to make the trip worthwhile. Just before I went to the High School, however, my dad gave me the money to fix myself up with a fountain pen and suggested Webberley's was the best place to get it.

The moment the bus dropped me off outside Woolworth's I knew I was going to be side-tracked. Pens were fine in their way, but not half as exciting as the cock loft, perched on a veranda above the stalls in Hanley Market. The Market Hall itself was a formidable structure occupying one side of the square and a sizeable chunk of the land behind it. Like its Tunstall counterpart, the ambience unwittingly created by its Victorian designers persisted. Its slabbed floor echoed to sellers' shouts and bargain-hunters' demands, to the clatter of crates and the shuffle of feet.

But it was the intermittent barks from above which provided the counterpoint to the noises below and announced the cock loft's claim to be the premium pet provider in the Potteries. Now I was treading the first step on my way to see what there was to see under those ornate wrought iron arches. Not that I was going to buy anything. After all, I was committed to my pen. But there was much to look at and Hanley was the place where you looked.

You could hardly call the cock loft spacious, but somehow puppies, rabbits, hamsters, kittens and birds managed to share the enclosure with sellers and purchasers, many of whom had made the trip by bus with no other intention than to buy an albino rabbit. I fancied a rabbit too, although all I knew about them was that they were partial to dandelions and sometimes put paid to their young. There were many examples that day in the cock loft, but the jingle in my pocket had to be resisted and before long I left for the museum.

At the time, this occupied an upper floor of the old Technical and Art Museum in Hanley's Pall Mall. You couldn't mistake it. A penny farthing could already be glimpsed through the window, and there were other discoveries to be made inside. The building itself was a museum piece, the rooms fusty, the stairs creaking, and its days were already numbered by the new showpiece about to be built a few hundred yards away.

Now I was climbing another staircase. Greeted by ammonites and a stuffed stoat, a case of crawlies and another of tyggs, those long-dead benefactors must have had a field day sifting through their attics secure in the knowledge their collection of moths would enter immortality via the city council and visitors like me, who should by now have been heading home with a new pen.

Not just yet. There was still one must-see left to see. Piccadilly would now seem an odd venue for a car dealership, but Pepper's, a garage specialising in MGs, didn't see it that way then. In a post-war world starved of panache, its sports cars, gleaming red and green behind the plate glass, cocked a snook at the rubbernecking wannahaves like me, whose wealth extended no further than the cost of a pen and the fare home. Those seductive curves, for the time being at least, would outrank Marilyn's.

I wrenched myself away and sauntered up to Webberley's without further side-tracking. Now for the pen. I examined the cabinets and counted my cash. I narrowed down my choice. Waterman, Conway Stewart or Parker? I went through my reserves a second time, pointed to a sleek black number. The girl took it out.

'Is it easy to fill?'

She was hardly likely to say no. It was a lame question anyway.

'I'll take that, then.'

'The Parker 51,' she said, wrapping it up. 'We sell a lot.'

I slipped the box into my jacket and made my way to the bus stop. As the double-decker drew up, I had a last thought: wouldn't I have been better off with the rabbit - or a pair of winceyette pyjamas

A face in the crowd. Morning Assembly.

3. REBRANDING

Chawner's, the Hope Street outfitter which supplied my school uniform, knew a thing or two about conformity. I went there with my mother to collect a blazer and flannels ready for the approaching term. The trousers had to be grey and the blazer navy blue. Black was tolerated so long as the crest, that all important emblem which stamped you forever a Hanliensian, was conspicuous on the breast pocket.

Resplendent in gold thread, surmounted by a griffin and bearing Victoria Regina's initials, the badge seemed too ostentatious to be taken seriously, despite its embroidered motto *Altiora Etiam Petamus* - Aim Ever Higher. I was already a marked man. From the moment it adorned my blazer, my pass had been stamped and entry gained. Chawner's also did a line in scarves and caps, for which money was somehow found.

I'd got the pen and the outfit. Now for the satchel and a starter kit to cram into it. The aim of the satchel was to make its wearer seem impressive as he struggled to cram the accordion of sleeves with a range of texts that would shame the local library. They came in various sizes, the capacious leather varieties costing more than the modest version which came my way. Then it was back to Webberley's for the Maths box, a hinged tin with its protractor, compass, dividers, HB pencil, 6" rule and square.

Two weeks ago I'd left the Nissen huts behind and taken my first steps into an unknown world. I'd shortly be catching the free school bus at the bottom of Sprink Bank Road to make the daily journey to the new school at Bucknall, leaving the huts to their fate and the old Grammar School buildings at Chell to the Secondary Modern pupils. Within a few years it would become a Junior High School, in a further metamorphosis, James Brindley High.

I took a bus to look at my new school before the term started. Beyond the main gates at Corneville Road lay an impressive arch, beyond that a wing in yellow brick and glass. I would soon become familiar with the rest of this enormous building, testimony to a system whose days were numbered before the cement was dry. For even before I walked through the gates, unseen forces were at work. A decade later, a government whose aspirations for bright working class children had produced such monuments would recoil in horror as it became apparent that, as well as giving people like me a chance, they'd unwittingly created what they saw as a new elite.

American style comprehensives, already burdened with problems in their country of origin, were about to be exported here - thus depriving both the academically gifted and the less academic their time of content at one fell swoop: the bright, because they enjoyed academic rigour; the less academic, because the paternalism which had nurtured Secondary Modern pupils - me included - worked best in the small, intimate and practical schools swept away under the guise of egalitarianism.

But what does a newly-blazered 13-year-old boy know of that, one of many cherry-blossomed and occasionally Brylcreemed standing in the mote-speckled shafts thrown across the assembly hall? The air smells of beeswax and the doors have been thrown open to admit the early-autumn air. That's what I know. I'm a face in the crowd, not much more than that.

A piercing shriek brings our murmuring to a close. Deputy Head 'Froggy' Marshall, looking like some languid and debonair English film actor, removes the whistle from his mouth and chides us from the side of the stage.

'Quietly, now, boys. Sit quietly.'

Dr Gardner now makes his entrance, his gown displaced from a shoulder, a hymnal and papers crooked under an arm.

'Good morning, school.'

'Good morning, sir.'

'Turn to hymn number 587: *He Who Would Valiant Be*'

The Bechstein thunders an introductory bar, and we rise as one.

> *He who would valiant be*
> *'Gainst all disaster,*
> *Let him in constancy*
> *Follow the Master.*
> *There's no discouragement*
> *Shall make him once relent,*
> *His first avowed intent*
> *To be a pilgrim....*

We take our seats in unison as a Sixth Former steps up to the lectern. A King James Bible lies open at the page, and he addresses the hall with the confident air of a public speaker.

'This morning's reading is taken from Ecclesiastes, Chapter 3, verses 1 to 9. To everything there is a season, and a time to every purpose under the

Heaven: a time to be born, and a time to die; a time to plant, and a time to pluck up that which is planted; a time to kill, and a time to heal; a time to break down, and a time to build up; a time to weep, and a time to laugh; a time to mourn, and a time to dance; a time to cast away stones, and a time to gather stones together; a time to embrace, and a time to refrain from embracing; a time to seek, and a time to lose; a time to keep, and a time to cast away; a time to love, and a time to hate; a time for war, and a time for peace. What profit hath he that worketh in that wherein he laboureth? Here endeth the reading.'

We remain in respectful silence, the words poorly understood, recalled in patches. Froggy rises to his feet.

'Our Father-'

We bow our heads in prayer, the familiar words meant and unmeant, part supplication, part ritual, spilling across the rows and aloft to the empty gallery. Then that steady declension of tone which signals the end. The Book of Common Prayer is marked at yesterday's page and tomorrow's and we know the passage as well as his plea before school lunch for the Lord to make us Truly Thankful.

'O Lord our Heavenly Father, Almighty and everlasting God, who hast safely brought us to the beginning of this day: Defend us in the same with thy mighty power: and grant that this day we fall into no sin, neither run into any kind of danger; but that all our doings may be ordered by Thy governance, to do always that is righteous in Thy sight; through Jesus Christ our Lord. Amen.'

'Amen.'

Cranmer's sublime words ring down the years; we Plough the Fields and Scatter, Hail the Power of Jesus' Name, Walk Upon England's Mountains Green. Within a few years Dr Gardner will die from a heart attack on a French beach; the Russians will launch their Sputnik; gowns, blazers and their crests will fade into the ether and the school will be rebranded Reginald Mitchell High.

A new phase in my life had begun.

4. WIELDING THE WILLOW

I was never properly introduced to Sandy, though I knew some who'd made his regular acquaintance. He'd not only history, but fame, too. By the time I got to hear of him, he'd long since earned his credentials.

He was always on hand in the gym when justice needed to be dispensed and was an uncompromising settler of scores. His once-varnished face had faded to a dull sheen, his handle constantly thickened by new tape, his time at the crease a distant memory. But he'd given sterling service over the years and never seemed to resent his descent from the Gentlemen's Game to a short length of willow wielded against an offending bottom. For Sandy, the sawn-off cricket bat, had been the choice of two generations of PT staff when doling out punishment to the recalcitrant.

He performed his duty without complaint and should have been awarded an MBE, if not a knighthood, for services rendered. Trial by medicine ball or enforced dangling from the wall bars might have had something going for them, but they lacked Sandy's prestige. Never being at the receiving end of him in full swing, one felt somehow impoverished. Canes and slippers were anonymous, whereas Sandy had charisma and a name to go with it.

The three games masters I remember are Les Morris, Dennis Wilshaw and Norman Downs. Square-jawed Les Morris, a kindly man, later left to work with disadvantaged children; Dennis Wilshaw also played football for England, scoring four goals when his country beat Scotland 7 - 2 at Wembley in 1955; Norman Downs was a tough all-rounder who took no prisoners and didn't suffer fools gladly. Sandy was to be found within an arm's length of all three, and the temptation to make use of him must at times have proved too strong to resist.

I once came within a hair's breadth of Sandy's kiss. PT lessons could take the form of games - football, cricket or shinty - athletics, gymnastics or cross-country running. Choice depended upon the teacher and the season. Today was a gym day. The vaulting horse had been carried in, the ropes and their occupants were dangling, a group were doing somersaults. A ring had been set up in the changing rooms, and Roberts and Carr were sparring. The whistle was imminent: showers beckoned.

By the time I'd dressed, the bell had gone for the next lesson. The class dispersed and I was on my way out when I remembered I'd left my watch in the gym office, as advised to do by the PT staff. I didn't want to be late for Spanish, so I took my satchel and made my way across the gym floor to collect my Ingersoll.

I could hear Norman Downs and Les Morris talking behind the part-open door, so I gave a tentative rap and waited for one of them to call me in. The door opened, and behind it stood Mr Downs, clad, like his colleague, in one of those shapeless Fifties' track suits which might have been the inspiration for the Madness hit *Baggy Trousers* thirty years later.

He had a way of making you feel uncomfortable, even guilty, without actually saying anything. As he ran his pale eyes from my face to my feet and up again, I got the distinct feeling I'd done something wrong. When he spoke, it was in that ominous tone employed by the man ladling gruel when Oliver asked for more.

'You've come for your watch?'

He laid a significant emphasis on the last word. The watch my dad bought me for Christmas might not have been up there with Cartier, but it didn't deserve the opprobrium now seemingly heaped upon it by my games master.

'Yes, sir.'

His eyes travelled once more to my feet, and hung there for a moment before the reverse trip. 'You've crossed the gymnasium to collect your watch - WITH SHOES ON?'

This time I followed his enraged stare until it came to rest on my jutting size elevens and hung there. In the ensuing silence I suddenly became aware of my transgression. I'd broken a cardinal rule - never, ever cross the gym in outdoor footwear. The gym floor was hallowed ground. Polished and beeswaxed to within an inch of its wall bars, those foolhardy enough to risk leaving their footprints on it - let alone scratch it - would at best be condemned to the sort of verbal lashing I was about to get, at worst to a blind date with Sandy.

'Sorry, sir, I forgot.'

'You forgot. YOU FORGOT!?'

I adopted what I hoped was conciliatory body language, arms folded behind, back and head bowed so that the table to Norman's side now fell within my vision together with Sandy, who, as ever, was lying on it looking deceptively inactive and eager for trouble.

'Sorry, sir.'

'Is that all you can say?'

'No, sir. I mean, yes sir.'

'STOP BABBLING.'

For the first time he took his eyes off me and swivelled them towards the sawn-off cricket bat. The taped handle lay invitingly within reach, and his hand inched towards it. It was then Mr Morris, who'd been checking a locker at the far side of the room, came to my rescue. Addressing Mr Downs, he said: 'You haven't forgotten Newcastle High?'

His reference to the imminent arrival of a visiting team at first fell upon deaf ears. Norman's unwavering stare continued to fix me like twin halogen headlamps. Sandy seemed to edge towards his outstretched fingers. Then the words struck home and the hard line of his mouth slackened. Taking my watch from a recess behind the door, he held it out.

'Take it.'

'Thank you, sir.'

'Now get out of my sight.'

'Yes, sir. Thank you, sir.'

I turned to go.

'AND -'

I turned back.

'Never, ever let me see you cross the gym in shoes again. You can walk back in your stockinged feet and if I hear you've been late for your next lesson you'll be getting a dose of this next time we meet.'

We both looked towards Sandy, who, deprived of his quarry, gave a bitter smile. The door banged shut, I untied my shoes and carried them and my watch back to the changing room.

My class were filing into the next lesson when I tagged on. I'd made it with seconds to spare, and I was feeling pleased with myself. It had been a close call. I'd deprived Norman of a victim, and Sandy of his customer base. Or Mr Morris had, which was much the same thing.

But there was a hesitancy in my smirk. I might have had a school crest, but I'd never had Sandy - and Sandy was even more prestigious. Maybe I should have walked over the gym floor in studded boots.

After all, think of the acclaim.

5. SHIFTING SANDS

My new routine mirrored wider changes, both in the country and closer to home. As I was beginning my new school, my father was about to change his. Now he moved from his job at Chell Primary, where I'd learnt my playground drill from Mr Salmon six years earlier, and took up a new post at Cauldon Road Juniors in Stoke. This entailed a ten mile bus journey until, in 1958, he purchased his first car - a 1946 Austin 12 - and travelled there in style.

He was to remain at the school until his retirement in 1973, and never aspired to be anything other than a class teacher. Of that elusive *smorgasbord* of luck, persistence, drive, nepotism, ambition and talent which gets you to the top, he had only the latter, knew it and knew it was not enough.

The Bush was not enough, either, for the 12" Bakelite television which arrived in time for the Coronation relegated our wireless to the second division. At first dad wasn't sure what to do with this new, alchemic device, except to reserve the right to switch it on and off - in itself a task shrouded in mystery. The shopkeeper had already warned us we couldn't expect instant results, and we gathered in cross-legged anticipation before a blank screen, waiting for the tilting tower which would herald this latest world of wonder.

To savour the delights of Coronation Day, however, the set had to be visible to the dozen or so awe-struck contestants taking refuge from the showers which had marred the best the Coronation Events Committee could do. My father's solution was to hoist the set onto a small wicker side table, itself precariously balanced on the chrome dressing table bought for my parents as a wedding gift before the War.

This eccentric arrangement drew no expressions of surprise. Maybe we thought this was normal practice, as we watched the golden coach drizzle through the London streets. Our televisual life began there. We'd been ushered into an idiosyncratic world far from the backs, where the news was read by a man in a tuxedo or a woman in evening dress, where a bell sounded half way through the drama, where hands at the potters' wheel or shires at the plough filled gaps in transmission in much the same way we'd filled the Ritz with howls of protest when the film broke.

Luckily, five decades were to elapse before the advent of Trash TV, where the glottal-stopping presenter who spends most of the time presenting him/herself rather than the subject is set running before the camera in a desperate attempt to generate 'mass appeal'. No gimmicks were needed to generate it in the Fifties. They'd have been hard put to match the *Quatermass Experiment*, that spell-binding Sci Fi I first saw in 1953, or George Orwell's distopian *1984*, with Peter Cushing as Winston. Or *Dixon of Dock Green*, or *Billy Bunter of Greyfriar's School*, or *The Grove Family at Home*.

There was much to laugh about, too, and comedians were free to be funny. Arthur Askey, Tony Hancock, Bob Monkhouse and Dennis Goodwin were among the participants that kept me in after homework, while Terry Thomas's gap-toothed toff ('Are you terribly well? Are you? Good show!) was as welcome in our living room as naturalists Peter Scott and Armand and Michaela Denis. Together they provided a comprehensive entertainment untroubled by the demands of a hundred-channel media circus, every frame a re-affirmation of a shared national identity which had existed for more than a thousand years and has been snuffed out in little more than a decade.

The Bush my father had carried home on his knee from Tunstall had indeed had its nose pushed out, but it hadn't entirely been displaced. We never seemed to have got around to owning a gramophone and apart from the park band, music had been supplied via our current wireless and its accumulator-driven predecessor. Now patriotic addresses were interspersed with Eric Coates' marches, which would later in the decade be eclipsed by hits from the parvenu Radio Luxemburg.

Before rock 'n' roll crashed through the glass ceiling of post-war musical taste, ballads poured from the Bush on our sideboard. Lita Roza's jokey *How Much is that Doggie in the Windo*w, Frankie Lane's soulful *I Believe*, David Whitfield's plea to *Answer Me*, Guy Mitchell's jaunty *She Wears Red Feathers* were sung in snatches by builders on their scaffold and window-cleaners on their rounds. Such offerings and Mantovani's strings were about to be eclipsed by Eddie Calvert's trumpet sobbing *Oh Mein Papa* and Johnny Ray sobbing over *Such a Night*. While Elvis was still driving a Memphis truck, Frank Sinatra, Dean Martin, Jimmy Young, Dickie Valentine, Tony Bennett, Slim Whitman, Alma Cogan, Ruby Murray and Winifred Atwell at her honky-tonk piano could all be found doing their bit most weeks.

Despite the imposition of homework - something I'd not been used to - I still found time to discover the joys of what my piano teacher sniffingly referred to as 'popular music'. Some of these three minute gems began to take their place alongside the easy classics I was playing at the time on the beery-toned piano acquired by my father. Rosemary Clooney's *Mambo*

Italiano, Dickie Valentine's *Finger of Suspicion,* Jimmy Young's *Unchained Melody,* Eddie Calvert's *Cherry Pink and Apple Blossom White* were hummed and whistled by postmen, milkman, Joe Mcgough as he delivered our coal and my mother as she clicked her needles. And me.

We were all caught up in these shifting sands and sounds. But a thirteen-year-old is at best a bystander, more concerned with steering clear of the gym floor than with those distant voices of change. What did it matter if the Mau Mau were flexing their muscles in Africa, that someone called Stalin had died in Russia, that John Kennedy had married someone in America? Was I any better off knowing Matthews had won his first FA Cup or that the ashes were back in England? What did the discovery of DNA and the unveiling of the new Ford Popular matter if a homework handed in late earned you a further essay from 'Tut' Smart?

The clock was ticking, but I never saw the fingers move. In hindsight, they covered quite a distance, and haven't stopped since.

Lita Roza

Me aged 15 with my sister Jacky.

September 1953, the new Hanley High School opens at Bucknall.

6. COSINES AND SIDEBURNS

And where was I when I wasn't globe-trotting? Appearing on the school photograph, where else? Photography had come a long way since Fox Talbot came up with the idea of the negative, but he'd stopped short of the digital camera with optical zoom and face detection you can now pick up at Argos for less than £50. So had our school photographer. Our photograph was more tripod and camera cape, with our man on guard to make sure the mechanism didn't pack in at this crucial moment in the calendar.

This was important if the session wasn't to be relegated to a risible place in school history. To produce the required print, the camera had to track in an arc from right to left, shooting each of the thousand faces as it went past. Usually everything went according to plan, but on occasions the temptation to appear more than once proved irresistible to some joker on the back row, who'd outrun the camera to materialise a second or, if he could manage it, a third time when the photograph came out. The result would be a visit to Dr Gardner, who had the unenviable choice of caning him for insubordination or awarding him a House Point for showing initiative.

It may well have been the former, for the Head, along with his unsuspecting staff, gardeners and caretakers were all sucked into the conspiracy once copies of the photo had been despatched and the culprit spotted. But the fuss would soon die down. The men sitting on the front row had seen active service a few years earlier; nothing that happened since could have the same impact - not even the serial appearance of a fifth form trickster on the official school snap.

All the teachers were male, a significant minority Oxbridge graduates. On my four-year journey through the school, I was taught by a fair cross-section and knew the ways of others through friends. There was one female in this vast tract of testosterone: Brenda Stanway, our glamorous blonde secretary, whose every moved was catalogued with the intensity of a paparazzo on the look-out for a scoop. Brenda was unnervingly cool, but I had the feeling that behind the inscrutable smile she enjoyed her lack of rivalry. She'd turn up unannounced on some errand or other which took her far from her office, her shoulder-length tresses shining and the usual female apparatus a rare treat as much for the blazered bored pouring over their cosines as their tweed-jacketed masters.

I had two English teachers during my time there. Sidney 'Tut' Smart - his nickname reputed to have arisen from his claim to have been in Egypt at the time of the discovery of Tutenkhamun's tomb - and 'Tich' Regan.

'Tut' was in his fifties then, a badger-haired smoothie at ease with his charges - though he had his side - and whose lessons were peppered with a breadth of vocabulary Shakespearean in range.

'I've noticed you seem to have taken more than usual care with your appearance recently, Peake. Could it be you're pursuing one of the fairer sex?'

'No, sir.'

'I hope you're not neglecting your lucubrations. I realise these other distractions can be very enervating.'

'What are lucubrations, sir?'

'Good Heavens, I'd no idea of the scope of your ignorance! The word's in common usage, boy. Your studies.'

'Why don't you just say 'studies', sir?'

'I despair. How will you ever learn? *Carpe diem*. I don't suppose you know what that means, either?'

'Is it something to do with fish, sir?'

'A loose translation would be 'seize the day'. I hope you will. What on earth is that elephantine racket outside in the corridor?'

'Tich' Regan's nickname was easier to pin down. Barely five feet tall, he tended to treat us with chilly reserve. He had a quick temper, and short shrift was given to those who fell short of his exacting standards. Once I found myself on the receiving end of this tongue when a piece of work I'd handed in was deemed lacking. My essay was pulled apart word for word - much to the delight of the class, who were the beneficiaries of ten minutes of free entertainment. It was 'Tich' who'd later prepare us for our Literature O-Level, which then required knowledge of a Shakespeare play, a work of fiction and an anthology of poetry.

I had the distinction of being in the lowest Maths' set, taken by 'Pongo' Hulme. Pongo's contribution to the lesson invariably took the form of a bored Robert Mitchum drawl, the words abbreviated as if giving them full weight demanded too much effort.

'An isosceles triangle: three corners: we'll call that li'll 'a', that's li'll 'b' and this li'll 'c'. Dissect it with a line. Big 'A' to Big 'C'. Base line 4.2cm. Angle at li'll 'b' 27. Construct the triangle. Three minutes.'

His unique shorthand took some getting used to, unlike Charlie Jackson's didactic style. Charlie, our other Maths master, a weighty, richly-toned man with a sharp wit, spelled it out and wrapped it up. I still couldn't climb the slippery slopes of algebra, calculus, trigonometry and geometry with ease, but at least my failures were more articulately brought home to me.

Sandy-haired Mr Boulton taught us Spanish. This fresh-faced wearer of rimless glasses was also known by his nickname 'Crowbait'. Legend had it that a pupil new to the school had been mischievously misinformed by the older boys that 'Crowbait' was the master's real name. When the boy was absent from school for a week, his mother's telephone message was received by none other than Mr Boulton himself:

'Is that Mr Crowbait, the Spanish teacher?'

'Yes, speaking....it's Mr Boulton, actually.'

Undeterred, the mother continued: 'I'm sorry my son won't be in this week, Mr Crowbait, only there's a bug going round and he's got it.'

'Thank you for informing me....actually, I'm Mr Boulton.'

'I shall have to go, now, Mr Crowbait, I'm already late for work.'

The Fifties was tentatively feeling its way towards the explosive Sixties. The private car, still a novelty on our estate, was already a familiar sight at school. Pongo's MG saloon, Dr Garner's Austin A70, Charlie Jackson's Citroen, Mr Tomlinson's Lambretta scooter and Micky Machin's derailleured bike could be found parked in the undercroft throughout the week. By 1955 my class of 13+ successes, 3R, had been split and moved into regular streams.

This paralleled less parochial movements elsewhere. Particularly in the roll-call of popular music, where Bill Hayley's *Rock Around the Clock*, unbeknown to him or us, had switched the punters to a new and exciting track which would influence styles to this day. While Dean Martin's memories were made of this and Anne Shelton was busy laying down her arms, artistes of a different stamp were already serenading us when we should have been paying attention behind our desks. Jerry Lee Lewis, Conway Twitty, Connie Francis, the Everley Brothers and, of course, Elvis, were knocking at the window and the neon lights were winking. Behind an armada of uplifted peneplains, Pitt's third Term, Keat's *Lamia*, Pongo's tangents and Crowbait's conjugations lurked a new world of flecked jackets and sideburns.

We all wanted some of that. We all wanted to be like Elvis. Even Elvis wanted to be like Elvis. We had bodily obsessions, too. Talk was more deltoids than Diogenes, our aim more bulging biceps than a bulging blonde. Lunch breaks were given over to the merits of weights, bench-presses, supplementary diets, training routines and Charles Atlas. The ratio of thigh to calf, waist to neck, chest to upper-arm dreamed up by some Greek narcissist three thousand years ago aroused strong passions. Magazines like *Health and Fitness* were always handy in someone's satchel. One devotee of body-building who'd actually managed to notch-up the sort of frame we all craved and wouldn't get would hold court over his acolytes:

'What size chest have you got, Ricky?'

'Thirty-eight. I put on another inch this year.'

'What method did you use, Ricky?'

'Bench presses with 40lb weights.'

'How many presses, Ricky?'

'Start with what you can manage and work up from there.'

'I'll get some weights and start tonight, Ricky.'

'You've got to stick at it. You can't afford to slack.'

'No, Ricky, I won't, Ricky.'

I couldn't afford the weights, so slacking was inevitable as far as I was concerned. It wasn't really my bag, anyway. I preferred to be out on my bike after the hour's homework we'd been set - though I did once have an adventure with a second-hand power spring.

Then, as O-Levels loomed, even that had to go.

An extract from the school photo.
I am in the third row from the back, 5th from the left with side-turned face.

7. PARTED CURTAINS

All this adventuring was getting to be a habit. Taking myself off to Hanley to explore the cock loft and purchase a Parker; risking cycle trips to such far-flung outposts as Freshwater; catching the train from Longport to Crewe so I could underline the numbers of the steam engines I saw there in my Ian Allan pocket book - blimey, if I went on at this rate I'd be taking over from Flash Gordon at the Chums' Club, fighting Ming the Merciless on Planet Mongo. And Flash had creepy Dr Zarkov to help when Flash was out of his safety zone. All I had was me and couple of friends who were just as naïve and we didn't have a ray gun between us.

Why should that put us off? We'd heard that Laurel and Hardy were appearing at the Theatre Royal in Hanley. Laurel and Hardy - in Hanley? This we had to see. Tickets were purchased, I've forgotten how, and we caught the bus in a fever of anticipation. An evening trip to Hanley was, by itself, several notches up in the sophistication stakes, but visiting a theatre unescorted by an adult, and wearing a tie to go there - that was a crossing of the Rubicon indeed. Our short trousers had long been cut up for dusters and we were now stumbling into the fleshpots of adulthood, even though they still seemed to come with a vanilla tub and Lucozade.

This was to be my first visit to the theatre, and I shuffled into my seat feeling both conspicuous and worldly and waited for the lights to dim. By this time, it would be around 1953, the famous duo were getting on. Those wonderful two-reelers which would later crop up on week-end television had long ago been sent to the cinema archive, but now here they were in person, treading the creaking boards of a Hanley theatre long after their expiry date. Did it matter? They still appeared in comic strips and their names still held enough cache to fill the seats. When the ensemble struck up that familiar jokey signature tune, perhaps it was curiosity as much as expectation that drew our eyes to the stage.

I don't recall much of their sketch, except that it involved a clash with the law and Hardy re-appearing in a well-torn suit, the result of a 'fracas' off stage. But I'd seen them, been there, done that, my first real-life sighting of those elusive people who only seemed to exist when the curtains parted and the lights came on.

There were many parted curtains after that. Barber's Palace and the Tunstall Ritz were still in the frame, but the frame had grown bigger and we'd grown bolder. Other lights were blinking from the 'what's on' columns of the Sentinel. Danilo, Gaumont, Roxy, Plaza, Rio, Essoldo, Regent, Capitol, Odeon, Majestic, Broadway, Empire, Coliseum - I was captivated by these glamorous titles, borrowed from ancient Greece or Rome or made up by a bunch of ad-men whose remit was to sprinkle a bit of stardust in our eyes at 1/6d a throw. These monumental art-deco palaces were the size of Zeppelin hangars and a world away from the bug huts and flea pits smelling of damp and Dettol which had evolved from some Victorian shed. Both marriage bureau and dating agency, only the hardiest could resist being swept from their mushy peas and brown sauce to this otherworld of soft lights, plush seats and usherettes done up like Munchkins.

Most capacious of all was the Palace in Hanley's Stafford Street. By the mid Fifties it had become the Essoldo, but the change of name did nothing to salvage its fortune, for in 1962 it had succumbed to the demolition ball. If size was what you were after, you need look no further than the Palace. The length of Harecastle Tunnel, large enough to have a weather system of its own, I once paid it a visit and spent the rest of the evening marvelling that a screen so distant could still be visible to the naked eye. Still, the girls with their long coats and bucket bags didn't seem to mind. Hair Armani-ed and high heels clicking, they were about to spend a couple of hours with Cary Grant - and who could blame them?

Hanley's Regent in Piccadilly was just as ostentatious, but in a different way. Between shows you were likely to be entertained by an organist at the Wurlitzer. And films weren't the only offering: an upper room also taught dance and was well attended by Fred and Ginger wannabes who swarmed up the steps on dance night.

We took the Burslem bus to see Elvis, who was starring in the film of the moment, *Love Me Tender*. This was playing to packed houses at the Coliseum. Bourne Bank might seem an unlikely setting for this Thirties extravaganza, tucked away from the main thoroughfare amid pot banks and bottle ovens, but the location must have had something going for it, for an equally enormous cinema, the New Ritz (formerly the New Palace) stood almost opposite.

The Coliseum, with its domed roof and porthole windows, thankfully lacked that distinctive odour which was the hallmark of its lesser brethren, apart from the smell of a swirling haze of cigarette smoke caught in the projection beams when the screen lit. None of this seemed to put off the courting couples in their double seats at the back. They were grateful for any venue that got them out of mother's parlour for an hour and who, as my hairdresser would later observe, were 'over each other like a rash'.

Barber's Picture Palace neither pretended to be one of those towering temples of excess, nor was it in the back-street league, where the seats came apart and the audience, rather than the film, supplied the entertainment. It was quirky in comparison, and the pencil-torched usherette made it her business to keep an eye on the fire door and a look out for the free-loaders whose mates inside had conveniently opened it for them. It was close to home, intimate, reassuring and a great springboard for adventures further afield.

Apart from the Regent, now a theatre and wonderfully restored to its art-deco glory - and the Odeon, situated just below where the Sentinel offices once stood - those weavers of dreams have been erased from the cityscape, if not from memory. The ghosts of the Essoldo might yet be hovering unseen above the shelves of Wilko's, which now occupies its site. And perhaps, at the time the final curtain would come down and we stood for the anthem, those living in the flats where Barber's Palace once enticed the Friday-night girls from their hearths and the lads from their pints might still, if they listen carefully, hear a voice calling 'Room for two at the back'.

Crowds at the Odeon, in Hanley.

8. WATER UNDER THE BRIDGE

I was due to sit my O-Levels in the summer, and there was more to life than examinations. I hadn't got the hang of girls yet, though, like Columbus, I suspected there was unexplored territory out there of which I'd shortly have sight.

My bike and I explored the Welsh Hills and made more than one trip to the Chester river-meadows. I tried my hand at roller-skating, and I managed to navigate the sprawl of Chatterley Whitfield Colliery on further cycling expeditions to the Roaches and Dovedale. Hanley still called, of course. Bottle-ovened, terrace-huddled, bright with lights, choirs, wrestling bouts, orchestras and ladies done up in their best, it seemed up-front, up-beat and up-market, an altogether more happening place than Tunstall. But this was a deception. Tunstall was just as sure of itself, but didn't like to brag about it. It was quieter there, the quietest place of all the library, where the only permitted sound was the rustle of newspapers turned by old men who'd congregate in the Reading Room to get from under their wives' feet for an hour.

Much had happened during my time at Hanley High School. Roger Bannister had run the mile in under four minutes, Donald Campbell had broken the water-speed record in Bluebird, Stirling Moss had won the Mille Miglia, Ruth Ellis had been sentenced to hang, Devon Loch had stumbled, Marilyn Monroe had married Arthur Miller and Nasser had seized the Suez Canal.

The old Potters' dialect - 'Can'st dew may a fayver?' 'Dust know wot tarm it is?' 'Er's just popped ite fer a bite'. 'Ast funt ite wee're it is yet, surry?' - showed no signs of flagging yet, but now it was interspersed with intrusions which had entered the country on the back of American pop. 'He's just crawled from under a stone.' 'Drop dead!' 'See you later, Alligator' were not only plucking at the local brogue, but ousting our home-grown slang.

I still remembered my flop at Chell Heath Juniors. Was I as cavalier as I'd been as a child of eleven, tugging my home-made kite through the steam as I raced the clanking colliery trains? I couldn't be sure. Who'd design a flow-chart directing me to that special job, tailored just for me? Who'd offer me advice - and if they did, would I take it? My plan only went as far as the books on the bed. After that it was in the lap of the gods.

'You want to take a break,' my mother would warn as I turned again for the stairs. 'You know what they say: all work and no play makes Jack a dull boy.'

'Jack didn't do O-Levels.'

'I can't see why you have to work every night. That's what they call burning the midnight oil.'

'I've got a lot to get through.'

I peered through the window at home-goers walking by in ones and twos, at the hill of grey waste rising behind the houses, at the pit chimney climbing the pale sky. Bedford vans and Foden lorries growled faintly through the pane. Strewn across the counterpane, a toppled tower of books and papers stared up at me. A sudden beam of late sunlight burnished the roofs. The street lamps would soon be lit. I needlessly smoothed the blanket, flipped through my notes. I found the page, took a deep breath, focused, read:

St Agnes' Eve, ah, bitter chill it was
The owl for all its feathers was a-cold
The hare limped trembling through the frozen grass
And silent was the flock in woolly fold....

Iambic pentameter, stressed syllable followed by an unstressed syllable in each metrical foot, five metrical feet, which gives Keats' poem its solemn resonance in keeping with its theme of troubled lovers.... the rhythmic pattern reinforces the initial imagery, which sets the scene for....

My eyes blurred. I suspect Keats had felt much the same, battling with his gift and his consumption in some airless hovel.

It was almost dark.

'Haven't you finished that by now?'

'I've only just begun.'

'I should give it a rest if I were you.'

The weeks unfolded. I garnered the last of a flotsam of facts and figures. Satiation paid me a visit, with its twin, lassitude. I didn't much care any more....

But now we're in the school hall with our Watermans, Parkers and emergency Quink. A clock is ticking from the stage. Folded question papers are placed with quiet precision on each desk. The fingers nudge the hour.

'You may begin.'

A rustle of papers, a spate of coughing. Pens are lifted, fiddled with, de-capped, re-capped and replaced as we struggle with the instruction. *You must answer four questions including at least one from Section.... no longer than 800 words....*

The lines haze, struggle for recognition, clear. The clock ticks unheard, the hall falls silent. Pens are raised, caps unscrewed, rulers already underlining the chosen question in blue-black. Someone coughs. A dropped pencil sounds suddenly loud in the room.

The holidays came, the bike wheeled out of the shed and oiled. I went to the Isle of Man. New adventures were being planned even as results time drew near. My false complacency began to wear thin. Now the hall tiles at home were examined daily, whatever was lying on the mat approached with trepidation.

And one day there it was, a pale manila envelope daring me to pick it up. I took it into the living room and laid it on the table. My father eyed me speculatively.

'You'd better open it.'

I tore at the flap, unfolded the list. I ran my eye slowly down the column.

'I've got all eight,' I managed, wondering if it had been sent to the wrong address.

My father took the paper. 'Well done.'

Struggling with vicarious pride, he went along to the pub at Riley Arms to celebrate.

None of my marks was outstanding. A quirk of the system, or a baffling self-revelation, was that my lowest mark was for English Literature. This must remain a puzzle, since a large part of my subsequent life has been spent writing books.

As my mother would say, 'It's all water under the bridge.'

She's right, of course. So where do I go from here? It's still a question I occasionally ask myself. Early the following year I seemed to have found the answer. I became a milkman.

And that's another story.

9. A LIFE OF RILEY

There was nothing politically correct about the Sixties. Life was something you laughed with or at, and practitioners of farce could be found everywhere. An example springs to mind.

As a boy, my brother Michael was the one who got his head stuck in the railings, was rescued from boats sinking in a foot of water, fell through the attic, shared a tunnel with a train and got locked in the store cupboard for cheeking the teacher.

The passage of time brought no improvement, but now he had wheels, and the possibilities of mishap loomed larger. One of his early purchases was a two-litre Riley. Once a fine saloon car, for some reason a previous owner had customised this model by removing the streamlined Riley front wings and substituting a couple of motor-bike mudguards. Perhaps he thought they'd give the car an 'edge'.

This was the sort of engineering that rang a chord with my brother. He parted with his cash and had one or two fairly successful years running the car around the City. However, the time came when the Riley ceased to give of its best. No amount of Saturday tinkering could reinstate its former performance. The decision was reluctantly made for it to go.

Mike's 'improved' Riley. Uncle Arthur admires the new mudguards

Michael made an attempt to coax the car as far as Longport, where the scrap man would hopefully buy it for a few quid. He set off feeling that he'd had the best out of the car, and now it was time to part. Unfortunately, the Riley had other ideas. As it travelled through Sandyford, it began to splutter and eventually came to a stop. For the time being, Longport was off the agenda.

He conferred with a companion what to do. He didn't want the car any longer, and he'd no money for repairs. It was then he had a bright idea. Near Summerbank School was a marl hole. He decided he'd push the Riley over the top. They waited for a lull in the traffic and heaved the car over the road and onto a track which led to the quarry.

Michael made a quick inspection of the drop. At around 80 ft and with a deep pool at the bottom, it seemed he'd hit on the right place. He got back in the car and they both began to push. Not far from the rim, they gave up. The track was becoming increasingly uneven. Michael doubted they'd ever achieve their goal. The pushing was heavy going, and he wondered vaguely if the car would start. After all, it had spluttered on for some time whilst on the main road. Even allowing for the fact it had come to a halt, might this not be a mere blip?

Leaving the door open, he got in and switched on. The engine burst instantly into life. He yelled to his friend to find a rock to pin down the accelerator while he kept the engine revved up. His impulse now was to jam the pedal, let out the clutch and leap away as the car travelled solo to extinction.

A large, flat stone was found and the scheme was up and running. Michael put the car into gear, trapped the accelerator under the stone, let out the clutch and sprang into the mud. The car moved to the rim of the marl hole and stopped. It had run out of petrol.

At that moment a stranger appeared and began to chat about the merits of a two-litre Riley. In passing, he asked my brother what he intended to do with the car.

'Well, tipping it over the edge springs to mind.'

The man reached into his pocket, took out a ten pound note and handed it over. 'I'll buy it from you, mate. I've always wanted one of these.'

My brother and his friend watched the man climb into the car and try to re-start it. He was still trying when they set off back home. A few months later Michael saw it again. Newly painted and with a pair of original mudguards in place, maybe he'd had the worst of the deal after all.

Adapted from the article by Bill Ridgway in *The Way We Were*, No: 98 October 2003

10. A BIZARRE FORTUNE

Nora counted herself lucky to get the job at Newport China. Not only were jobs hard to come by in the early Thirties, but the work was convenient. She wouldn't have to waste her money on bus fares. Instead, she only had a short walk from her Middleport home to the factory. She'd use the canal. The towpaths could get a bit mucky at times, but in the summer there wouldn't be any problems.

The job was nothing grand. It mainly involved packing orders in crates, using handfuls of straw so the stuff wouldn't get smashed. She'd done similar work before. You could learn it in a day.

The following Monday she set off at 6.30 in the morning. It would only take about a quarter of an hour to get to the factory, plenty of time to clock on and get her bearings before a 7am start. She walked past a couple of chugging barges and breathed in the fresh morning air. She didn't feel in the least nervous starting at Newport. She'd heard it was a good firm to work for. After all, it was her next door neighbour who'd put in a word for her, so she had it straight from the horse's mouth.

She recognised one or two faces as she went in, among them Alf Dunkerley, the gate man who lived down her street. She gave him a nod and they exchanged a pleasantry as he directed her to her section.

She worked in the packing shop with half a dozen other girls. Soon they were chatting away as they stacked the wares in crates ready for carting off. Today they were handling domestic china - cups, saucers and plates. Every so often the foreman stuck his head around the door, but by and large they were left to themselves.

Nora found the work dull and repetitive. But it was money, wasn't it? No good complaining. And at least the stuff she was packing was attractive. Not like the crocks they had at home, heavy white earthenware with chips and crazes defacing every piece. No, she was handling bright, colourful ware - vases and the like, with bold, unfamiliar designs which made them stand out in the gloom of the shed.

One particular item took her fancy. It was a bowl with what looked like yellow meadows in which stylised daisies grew. There were trees, too, with black trunks and umbrellas of dense orange and green foliage. She spent a minute looking at it before shrouding it in straw and packing it in with the rest.

'You like that, do you, Nora?' said Gladys, jamming the top on. 'It's all the rage, so they say. I can't see the point myself. It's too much, isn't it? Too jazzy. I like stuff that's plain. This is like a dog's dinner. Still, somebody must like it. This is the fifteenth crate we've shipped off to London in the last three days, and none of it comes cheap.'

'Whoever did it must have a vivid imagination.'

'It's that new paint shop woman, Miss Cliff. Clarice. She's made an impression on the boss, they say. He gave her the go-ahead to use some old pots to experiment on. Now she's in charge of a team. She turns out a new line every week, I'm told. Anyway, time to knock off. See you tomorrow.'

Next day nobody noticed Nora had a bigger work bag, with capacious pockets and a compartment inside for holding bulky items like a loaf of bread. She took pains to place the bag just under the packing bench, so that to all but the most observant, it was out of sight.

She got on well with the girls and the day went quicker than before. In fact, it didn't seem any time at all before the hooter sounded and they were reaching for their coats.

'Coming my way, Nora?' Gladys called.

'You go on, duck, I'll catch you up. I'll just crate up these last half dozen vases before I knock off. Don't worry, I'll soon be done.'

'Suit yourself. I must say, you're a glutton for punishment.'

The packing shop was empty. Quickly, Nora took the vase from the bench and looked around. She could hear home-going voices outside. Her heart was pounding as she quickly scooped up a vase and slid it in a bread wrapper she'd brought in her bag. She pushed the package into the large compartment, picked up the bag and walked out into the late afternoon sunshine. She smiled at Alf as she went through the gates and he nodded in return. Gladys was just ahead, and she waited for Nora to catch up. They walked as far as the tow path, then parted company.

When Nora reached home, she set the vase on the table. Her husband Jack was up at his mother's and wouldn't be back until late. That was good. She didn't want any awkward questions until she'd thought up a plausible answer. It was still there as she ate her tea. Afterwards, she took the step ladders from the spare bedroom and climbed up with her package into the loft. Carefully she stowed the vase behind the chimney. She looked at it in the dim light for a moment before making her way back down.

Before the year was out, Nora had stolen - though she preferred to use the word 'collected'- an entire dinner service. It all depended on what came down the line. She learnt the other girls' habits - who came, who went, and grew more confident in her secret pursuit. She was never greedy. When cups and saucers had to be packed, she'd never take home more than one of each in any one day. Well, two at the outside. Sometimes she had a struggle. Some items were large, like the Inspiration vase she felt inspired to take last Friday, but she'd mastered her craft. Alf kept smiling at the gate and she kept smiling at Alf as she walked by with her bag.

She became obsessed. An alien part of her was taking over. Her hands seemed to have a will of their own. By now ware was spilling across the attic and she had to hide her hoard under old coal sacks. Soon she was forced to hide it in the gaps between the joists, and cover it with oddments of linoleum and old newspapers. By the following Christmas, cups, saucers, plates, a range of *Bon Joir* tea sets, vases, bowls, figures of jazz musicians, egg cups and sugar dispensers all lay buried under a layer of dust.

Over the years Jack and her daughter Anne had grown blind to what they saw as her mother's eccentricities. Jack had died in 1978 and Nora, now well into her 80s, plodded on for a few more years. She spent much of her time dozing and sometimes vivid dreams of her far-off time at Newport China would wake her with a start.

A fatal stroke put an end to all that. It fell upon Anne and her son Joe to sort out her mother's effects. It took weeks to clear out the rooms, and Anne left the loft till last. Her torch picked out the rafters and joists and the dusty coverings between them. She lifted a yellowing newspaper and coughed in the rising flurry of dust. Her fingers touched a bowl and she drew it out. Childhood memories flooded back. Now she could recall her mother appraising those gaudy pieces under the landing light before making a furtive trip up the ladder. There'd always been an air of mystery about them, as if they shouldn't really have been in the house at all. Her mother had always said they were cheap seconds, she'd got them for next to nothing, and she 'might get them down and make a show one day'.

But that was then and this was now. It took hours for Anne and Joe to bring all the stuff down and to pile it in tiers across the living room floor and table. She had hated them as a child, and hated them still. All those crude orange smudges and startling blues and greens and those ridiculous trees. Whoever saw a teapot shaped like a slice from a Swiss roll? Whoever heard of a cup handle you couldn't lift the cup by. They would have to go. They were all bizarre.

They had some trouble getting the ware into the van Joe had hired from his boss, and they had to make several journeys to the tip before the job was done. Anne watched with satisfaction as a lorry disgorged its cargo of waste over the hideous cups and saucers, over the brash plates and flashy vases. Now they'd vanished from sight. Now she could get on with selling her mother's house.

Twenty years later, Anne found herself paying a visit to the dentist. Appointments were running late, and being the sort of woman who got bored if she was doing nothing, she began to thumb through a magazine handy on the side table. An article on antiques caught her eye. Not her thing, but.... and she settled to read.

She didn't hear the receptionist call her name, for her eyes were sharply focused on the page. She felt faint. Staring her in the face was....

'Are you alright?'

She shook her head at the woman seated beside her. 'I'm alright. It's..it's....'

Her eyes were still glued to the page as she carried the magazine out of the waiting room and out into the street. Prices leapt up at her. Dinner sets and vases which now lay buried under tons of rubbish were worth - her mind clicked like a cash register. She'd buried the price of a country villa, perhaps a country estate. All those tasteless, trashy pieces were now sought-after items. *'Clarice Cliff's Bizarre range,'* she read through blurred eyes, *'is extremely collectable. Only last year, Southerby's sold an Inspiration vase for -'*

Ann gasped Crushed beneath 20ft of junk lay both her dreams and her answer to them. Reaching home, she went straight to the drinks cabinet.

'How did the check-up go?' her husband asked from behind his paper.

'I didn't bother. I didn't feel like it.'

He lowered his paper. 'You know, these house prices keep shooting up. We'll never be able to afford anything up-market now.'

'Oh, spare me!' his wife shouted, storming upstairs to bed and leaving him to peruse the rest of the news.

This item is adapted from Bill Ridgway's story *A Bizarre Fortune Buried at the Tip*, which appeared in the December 2003 edition of *The Way We Were*.

11. MOPS, SOCKS AND KING EDWARD'S

No other casual work presented itself after my delivery round escapade until, in 1956, I was offered a Christmas job working at Tunstall Woolworth's. This came via my aunt Dorothy, best friend of Eva Twigg, who worked there. Eva is one of a dwindling band of staff whose memory of the store stretches back into the war years, and I've since spent many idle moments talking with her about her time there. As a child, Woolworth's was on my mother's shopping round, the place where coupons were clipped and dolly mixtures forfeited. It has long held a place in my affections, and Eva's account of her work there provides a last glimpse into that now distant world. This is what she says:

'I started work on the toiletries counter, Department 22, on a wage of 19/8d a week. Hours were from 8.45am to 5.30pm Monday to Wednesday and Saturday. On Fridays you worked from 8.45am to 7pm, and Thursday was half day, closing at 1pm. You weren't entitled to a holiday for the first year of your employment, but after that you were allowed one week a year. It wasn't until the mid Fifties that you got a full two weeks off.

'It was January 2nd, 1942 when they set me on. I was just 14, the youngest in the store. The normal age for setting on was 18, but a lot of women were on munitions or the land army, so there was a shortage of labour and they had to lower the age limit.

'Because of labour shortages, you could volunteer to work in another Woolworth's store in your holiday week. I opted for Blackpool Woolworth's, and I went there with a girl from Longton to work in their café. You couldn't go on the beach because of all the barbed wire, and although Woolworth's paid your fare and board, you had to be in your digs by 9pm. There wasn't much food, either. Breakfast was two pieces of toast and a cup of tea, with sandwiches for your 6pm meal - fish and chips if you were really lucky.

'My job in Blackpool was to serve breakfast in the store café and clear the tables. We worked from 11am till 4pm, mainly serving US soldiers, because there was a US army base nearby. It might have been a break, but it was no holiday, and I didn't volunteer again.

'The manager when I first went to Tunstall Woolworth's was Mr Cyril Martin. He was a nice man, quite tall with thin, gingery hair. He'd have been in his 40s then. I worked under him for two years, then he went south to run a big store in Exeter because the manager there had been called up.

'I moved to department 19, selling cards. I was there for four years. There were no other card shops in town then, so I was kept busy - especially at Christmas and Easter. The problem there was finding an envelope to fit the card, especially with customers queuing.

'There were forty departments in Tunstall when I started. Bigger stores had more, and some had less. There were six island counters and three side counters on each wall with tills at the ends of each counter. When I first went there, the counters were made of mahogany, with understocks for your merchandise. We had to wash them down with water and vinegar every two weeks to make them shine. It wasn't until the Fifties that they were replaced by metal and glass counters. The island counters would have two or three departments, with two women serving.

'I soon learnt which department sold what, and I've mostly remembered to this day. Department 1 sold sweets, mainly Waller and Hartley. Walls ice-cream was sold on 2, and the wafers were 6d and a choc-ice 1/- when you could get it. No coupons were needed for ice cream. That was delivered in big blocks to the store around Friday tea-time, and there'd be queues all down the High Street, mainly workers from H and R Johnson and Richards' Tiles. We used cutters to make eight wafers per block. Sometimes they bought some chocolate ice cream in silver foil paper. The word would get out and there'd be even longer queues.

'Food was on Department 3. You had to bring your ration book or you weren't allowed anything. Most foodstuffs arrived in bulk, and had to be weighed before you sold them. Department 4 sold jewellery. Being wartime, identity bracelets were very popular, with your name and war-time number. My number was ONHJ/403/3. We engraved the numbers on a silvered steel plate with a drill.

'Biscuits were Department 5 - Elkes' - when you could get them. They were stored in a cardboard box and sold by weight. Sometimes there'd be a consignment of ginger nuts, custard creams, arrowroot, shortbread or chocolate wafers, but not often. Customers were allowed 1/2lb of biscuits each and they were on ration, like sweets. Broken biscuits were sold to regulars, sneaked across the counter, 1lb per person.

'Department 9 had men's socks, Lisle stockings, handkerchiefs and scarves. There were no women's nylons, though. If you wanted your legs to look pretty you'd need to dye them with coffee and use an eye-brow pencil to draw the seam. We never stocked coffee, so if you could get hold of some, that would be at the Home and Colonial in the Square.

Haberdashery was 15, which included darning mushrooms, Aero knitting needles, reels of cotton and measuring tapes. You could also get knitting patterns, but you couldn't get wool because of war regulations. Department 20 had stationery, and you bought books at 21. Fairy tales were always popular, and magic painting books where you applied water to the page and this activated the colours in the paper. I remember cut-out books were popular too, where you could cut out a figure and 'dress' her in cut-out clothes.

'The toy section also sold crayons and Plasticine. I remember Mr Martin once gave me the job of modelling some animals from a big slab of Plasticine and displaying them on a stand before Christmas. The Horticulture Department, no 32, was always busy. I was transferred there for a time after Mr Martin left for Exeter. People would buy seeds or potatoes. We sold King Edward's, Sharpe's Express and Arran Pilot potatoes and it was heavy work, a real maul. You had to take a handful out of the sack and weigh them out, and sometimes they were rotten. Every time we handed over a bag we'd say 'Dig for Victory'. The seeds were manly carrots, beans, cabbage and lettuce. We couldn't sell enough.

'Another big seller was enamelware, on Department 33: saucepans, plates and mugs. There was a delivery once a month by dray from Longport Station. It arrived at 8.30am, and half the girls had to climb up and unload it while the other half carted it away in baskets to the storeroom. It always came packed in straw, and you had that all over the High Street and in your hair as well. People got to know of a delivery down the grapevine and they were forming a queue while we were still unloading. Customers were allowed one plate and one mug each, but you had to keep your eyes peeled for some who tried to go around twice.

'The other departments I remember are household goods like mops, brushes and shovels at 34 and the electric counter, 26. They had light bulbs, flex and cable sold by the yard.

'Woolworth's was always busy. Cashiers came around three or four times a day to empty the tills. Each girl was responsible for the money in her till and it didn't have to be a farthing out or there'd be trouble. We'd have to work out a customer's change in our head, but if they'd had a lot of items we used pads on a string, which were kept by the tills.

'After the money was collected from the tills, there'd be a set of float bags containing three £1 notes and two 10/- notes, silver and copper. These were put into the tills next morning before opening. Rationing was a nightmare. Coupons had to be cut out of the ration book for the appropriate week with the scissors provided, and on occasions people would come in with half-a-dozen Ration Books for themselves, their grandma, grandad, Uncle Joe Cobley and all.

'Then they wanted $^1\!/_2$oz of this on one book and 1oz of something else on another - it was a nightmare. You quickly got to know how many coupons were needed for different items. One coupon was needed for 1oz of sweets or a small plain bar of Cadbury's. You had another nightmare at the end of the day, when all the coupons had to be taken to the cashier's office and counted before being sent off somewhere.

'After the war, Mr Martin came back and his Deputy was Miss Antrobus. She came from Alsager where she lived to Tunstall Station every day by train. Esme Dale was staff supervisor, who sorted out the girls and set them on. In the stockroom upstairs was the stockroom manager with four boys helping out. Another name I recall is Jeanna. For a time I shared a counter with her, selling ice cream and squash. The squash was in a container with a tap and water from upstairs was brought down in a bucket to dilute the juice. It was so weak it looked like coloured water. It sold well at 2d a cardboard beaker and we used to drink it at dinner time ourselves. One of the other things we sold was sheet music, at 6d, and this was advertised with a wind-up gramophone which drove me nuts because all they ever played was *My Mother Dun Told Me*. I don't think they had any more records.

'After Mr Martin left to work at Exeter, Mr Trow was the new manager for a time. He was at the store until 1944. He wasn't as easy-going as Mr Martin. If the girls spoke to each other he'd rap on the counter. When he left, Miss Antrobus became manager for a spell.

'What stays with me is the electric bell. It was always ringing, especially when you bagged up your takings. There was a bell to begin the day, a bell when the till bags came round, a bell when you had to fill your till bag and a bell when you had to take your till bag to the office. It was all synchronised, and anyone taking up their bag early or late got a telling off. The cashier would put the bags in a huge safe for the night. At 9am next day, the money was counted, the takings from each Department written down and the cash taken over to Barclay's Bank in two big bags by the Manager, his Deputy or the stockroom man. They'd take it at different times to avoid theft.

'At other times there'd be a bell for air raid drill. Customers were asked to leave by the Manager and the doors and tills were locked. All the girls then had to go into the courtyard at the back to have a register taken. In case incendiaries were dropped, there was another drill. This time we had to go through the stockroom -and usually it was dark- up a ladder on to the roof, then across the roof and down into another courtyard at the back of Home and Colonial.

'The cleaners all left for munitions work at Radway Green, which at £3 a week paid much better, and the girls had to take it in turns to mop out the kitchens, cloaks and laundry on Thursday mornings.

'In winter there were blackouts at the windows, with the gas lights turned down low inside. A first aid knapsack was kept handy, with bandages and iodine in it. We each had our own gas mask, too, kept in a cardboard box with string handles under the counters and taken everywhere you went - even up to the canteen. In 1943 we started to sell leatherette in different colours at 2/- a yard, and the staff would decorate their boxes with it. I covered my gas mask box in navy blue leatherette - a real fashion statement.

'The place was heaving, especially at week-ends, when we'd get US soldiers from Biddulph pulling up in jeeps and trucks outside. Then the war suddenly ended. We ran out of the store and waved our Union Jacks from the pavement. By then Mr Martin had taken over again as manager, and the celebrations didn't stop him trying to sell flags to passers-by at 6d a time. Someone had also gone into the stockroom and draped a huge Union Jack out of the window.

'Mr Martin put me on stocktaking upstairs, where we kept our merchandise. Each item had a slip and a number, with selling price and cost price. He checked that all the paperwork was correct, and I'd write it down in a ledger. After the war I carried on doing different jobs in the store, including taking stock after Boxing Day. That lasted seven days, working till 11pm. Then later I had to learn about income tax, graduated pensions and insurance when Margaret, the Head Cashier, was on holiday and I had to do all the staff wages. Margaret became a good friend.

'A lot of Woolworth's girls didn't marry. They were still working there right through the Fifties. But gradually things changed. We opened a deli counter, and began to get in fresh strawberries and peaches. Eventually the coupons went. By the early Fifties the new boss was a jolly Welshman, Mr Williams. He let us call each other by our first names for the first time. After him came Mr Moore, who was still there in the Sixties - the same time the first adding machines were introduced. Mr Moore died, and Mr McIntyre took over. He took early retirement the year before I left.

'My friend Margaret and I celebrated 21 years of service in 1963 and were given gold watches from Garrards. There was a big party in the Town Hall afterwards for family and friends. When I'd done 40 years, I was given £200 - but no party, because staff by now were depleted. A big change had set in after

Mr McIntyre started. Apart from new steel counters, the office moved upstairs and the space was made into a music room, selling records. There was only Margaret and me doing administration now, with a couple of supervisors and fifteen part time girls on the counters. We had to make our own tea and take sandwiches or walk over to the chip shop. The storeman was made redundant and I had to do his job, receiving goods - that was besides being Invoice Clerk and Assistant Cashier.

'We carried on until the Eighties, but a lot were taking early retirement with redundancy, so Mr McIntyre decided to take it and told us things were going to get worse and advised me to take it too if we were offered early retirement. Margaret and I retired in May, 1987. I was nearly sixty. The store closed two months later and Superdrug took over.

'I really enjoyed my time at Woolworth's. I'd worked there for forty-five years doing all sorts of jobs, ending in Assistant Cashier. They were good days, though I never got extra for the extra jobs I did. It's hard to believe that a household name like Woolworth's is all in the past now.'

Bill Ridgway interviewed Eva Twigg in July, 2009.

Margaret Mulroy and Eva Twigg notch up
21 years service at Tunstall Woolworth's 1963.